The Food Doctor

The Food Doctor

Healing foods for mind and body

Vicki Edgson DipION & Ian Marber DipION

C&B

COLLINS & BROWN

imprint

I wish to thank my parents, who brought me up to believe that anything is possible in life, if you're prepared to apply yourself to it. (Vicki Edgson)

I dedicate this book to my loyal family and friends and to all the people who have helped put this book together. (Ian Marber)

First published in Great Britain in 1999
by Collins & Brown Ltd
London House, Great Eastern Wharf, Parkgate Road, London SW11 4NQ

Distributed in the United States and Canada by Sterling Publishing Co,
387 Park Avenue South, New York, NY 10016 USA

9 8 7 6 5 4 3 2 1

British Library Cataloguing-in-Publication Data:
A catalogue record for this book is available from the British Library.

ISBN 1 85585 682 4

Design XAB Design
Photography Neil Mersh, Jo Henderson
Cover photography James Duncan
Editors Claire Hill, Fiona Corbridge

Colour reproduction by Media Print, England
Printed and bound in Hong Kong by Dai Nippon

SAFETY NOTE
The information in this book is not intended as a substitute for medical advice. Any person suffering from conditions requiring medical attention, or who has symptoms that concern them, should consult a qualified medical practitioner.

contents

introduction

' Our own relationship with food, health and vitality has changed enormously since we trained as nutrition consultants. We both feel ten years younger, and we're frequently told how well we look. By far the greatest change has been to our energy levels, which are now sustained throughout the day, keeping us enthusiastic and motivated. And we still enjoy an occasional glass or two of wine or a chocolate dessert – good health can afford the odd lapse without any serious repercussions!

If you are keen to know more about health and nutrition, this guide provides the basics, plus the latest research, in a concise, practical format. Part one deals with food and its effects on the mood and mind; part two tells you how to use nutrition to fight specific ailments. Together with advice on weight management, food allergies, cooking methods and a selection of delicious, health-boosting recipes, we are confident that our book will give you a better understanding of the role food has to play in your health and emotional well-being. '

IAN MARBER   VICKI EDGSON

www.thefooddoctor.com

lifestyle questionnaire

As nutrition consultants, we regularly find that clients come to us with the same problems, the causes of which are often not immediately apparent. For some ailments, over-the-counter remedies can be tried, however, these will not address the root causes of a problem: an investigation of the client's lifestyle is needed.

Listed below are the 20 health problems most frequently described by our clients. If you have a similar problem, refer to the relevant questionnaire. If you find that you answer 'yes' to most of the questions, we show you the possible underlying causes. For example, feeling tired all the time could be put down to the pressures of work or children, but if sugar and caffeine cravings are also experienced, it could indicate an allergy or yeast infection. The common denominator for many symptoms is the health and efficiency of the gut which, in turn, is closely linked to the liver and the pancreas. Encouraging the digestive system to become more efficient helps symptoms to improve within a relatively short period of time. Look up these problems in the others chapters of this book where they are discussed more fully. Bear in mind that the causes listed here are possible causes, and are not intended as a substiture for advice from your doctor.

1 LACK OF ENERGY/ FATIGUE

Questionnaire

- Do you feel tired all the time?
- Are you irritable and snappy?
- Does sleep leave you unrefreshed?
- Do you feel drained mid-afternoon?
- Do you often feel unwell for no apparent reason?
- Is your intake of sugar, tea and coffee high?

Possible causes: gut permeability and food allergies, gut dysbiosis and yeast overgrowth, toxic metals, low blood pressure, low thyroid function, limited diet and poor blood-sugar management, nutrient deficiencies.

2 PAIN AND INFLAMMATION

Questionnaire

- Do you get arthritic pain in any joints or digits?
- Are any joints swollen?
- Do you have much neck, shoulder, or back pain?
- Are most of your meals fast food?
- Do you use non-prescription painkillers, such as Ibruprofen, daily?

Possible causes: food intolerances, gut dysbiosis and yeast overgrowth, deficiencies of essential fatty acids, auto-immune disease, thyroid imbalances, physical injury, impaired detoxification by the liver.

3 INDIGESTION

Questionnaire

- Do you often get stomach pains after eating?
- Are you frequently constipated?
- Do your stools contain partly undigested foods?
- Do you suffer from bouts of belching?
- Do you regularly chew gum?

Possible causes: low level of stomach acid, lack of digestive enzymes, bacterial infections and parasites, food intolerances, gastric or duodenal ulcer and frequent use of antacids, impaired liver function.

4 GAS AND BLOATING

Questionnaire

- Do you feel bloated immediately after eating?
- Is gas frequently a problem?
- Do you often get abdominal cramps?
- Are you a regular alcohol drinker?
- Do you crave sweet foods, bread, pasta, or wine?

Possible causes: low level of stomach acid, lack of digestive enzymes, bacterial/parasitic infections, food intolerances, poor elimination, poor food choices.

5 HEADACHES AND MIGRAINES

Questionnaire

- Do you regularly take painkillers for headaches?
- Do you eat lots of cheese/chocolate/dairy foods?
- Are the above more acute at menstruation?
- Have you any food allergies?
- Do you experience digestive problems?

Possible causes: food intolerances, gut permeability, toxic metals, vasoconstriction attributable to smoking, alcohol, blood-sugar mismanagement, postural misalignment or injury, visual impairment.

6 PMS

Questionnaire

- Are your periods irregular?
- Do you crave chocolate before a period?
- Are you irritable, intolerant, or anxious prior to menstruation?
- Do you suffer from weight gain or water retention each month?
- Do you experience premenstrual cramps?

Possible causes: magnesium and vitamin B6 deficiencies, poor circulation, hormonal imbalances, pituitary hormone imbalances, stress.

7 ANXIETY AND NERVOUSNESS

Questionnaire

- Do you always imagine the worst?
- Have you got many fillings in your teeth?
- Were you brought up in an industrial area?
- Do you crave sugar and sweet foods?
- Do you consume soft drinks and caffeine daily?

Possible causes: toxic metals and environmental pollutants, brain chemical imbalances, amino acid imbalances, impaired liver function, food intolerances, yeast overgrowth, stress.

8 DEPRESSION

Questionnaire

- Are you an irregular eater?
- Do you use food to alleviate the blues?
- Are you a heavy smoker or drinker?
- Do you lack motivation?
- Do you experience problems in sleeping?

Possible causes: blood-sugar mismanagement, toxic metals and environmental pollutants, brain chemical imbalances, bacterial and yeast overgrowths, gut dysbiosis, food intolerances, stress, family history, recreational drug abuse.

9 HIGH BLOOD PRESSURE OR HIGH CHOLESTEROL LEVEL; CHEST PAIN

Questionnaire

- Do you suffer from palpitations?
- Are you out of breath after climbing the stairs?
- Do your hands or feet tingle?
- Do you add salt during cooking and to meals?
- Are you a smoker?
- Are fried foods a major part of your diet?
- Are you more than 10 kilos (22 lb) overweight?

Possible causes: lack of exercise, nutritional deficiencies, diet high in saturated fat and fried foods, low thyroid function, adrenal stress, smoking, excessive alcohol consumption, high salt intake, heart disease.

10 DIABETES (TYPE II – MATURITY ONSET)

Questionnaire

- Do you eat a lot of sweet snacks?
- Do you experience mood swings during the day?
- Are you frequently irrational and argumentative?
- Are you thirsty all the time?
- Do you urinate frequently?
- Are you constantly tired?

Possible causes: pancreatic insufficiency (lowered insulin production), high carbohydrate diet, lack of digestive enzymes, obesity, lack of exercise, impaired liver function, adrenal stress, chromium and vitamin B3 deficiencies.

11 INFERTILITY (male and female)

Questionnaire

- Have you been trying to conceive for more than one year?
- Do you drink alcohol regularly?
- Are you under a lot of stress?
- Do you eat a lot of fast or convenience foods?
- Do you live in a highly polluted area?

Possible causes: hormonal imbalances, bacterial and parasitic infections, toxic metals and environmental pollutants, specific nutrient deficiencies (essential fatty acids, magnesium, zinc, some amino acids), food intolerances, physical obstructions.

12 ALLERGIES

Questionnaire

- Do you get hayfever or a runny nose (rhinitis)?
- Do you have frequent headaches?
- After eating, do you get palpitations?
- Are you experiencing skin irritation?
- Do you crave specific foods?
- Do you often feel depressed?

Possible causes: gut dysbiosis and permeability, vaccinations, environmental pollution, poor liver function, imbalance of essential fatty acids, adrenal stress, low level of stomach acid, lack of digestive enzymes.

13 SKIN PROBLEMS

Questionnaire

- Have you travelled a lot recently?
- Is your skin irritated by heat or direct sunlight?
- Are you under a lot of stress?
- Do you regularly drink alcohol?
- Do you eat a lot of dairy or convenience foods?
- Do you eat any of the same foods every day?

Possible causes: food intolerances (specifically dairy, wheat and citrus), hormonal imbalances, parasitic infections, deficiencies in essential fatty acids, vitamin C deficiency, junk-food diet.

14 ECZEMA AND ASTHMA

Questionnaire

- Is your diet high in fried foods and red meat ?
- Do you eat dairy produce daily?
- Are you drinking alcohol on a regular basis?
- Are you on any prescription or over-the-counter medication?

Possible causes: food intolerances (especially dairy, wheat and citrus), imbalance of essential fatty acids, poor posture, allergy to cosmetics and cleaning agents, diet high in saturated fats.

15 HYPERACTIVITY

Questionnaire

- Do you eat a lot of sweet foods?
- Are convenience or ready meals a major staple?
- Do you drink coloured soft drinks and sodas?
- Are you already on medication for hyperactivity?
- Do you regularly take aspirin?

Possible causes: food allergies and intolerances, sensitivity to food additives, salycilate sensitivity (aspirin-like compounds found in certain foods) deficiency in essential fatty acids, environmental pollutants and toxic metals, vaccinations.

16 DIARRHOEA/CONSTIPATION

Questionnaire

- Do you suffer from alternate bouts of diarrhoea and constipation?
- Is your diet low in fruit and vegetables?
- Do you hardly ever exercise?
- Are you taking any over-the-counter painkillers?
- Are you using laxatives?

Possible causes: gut inflammation and permeability, diet low in fibre, lack of exercise, bacterial/parasitic infections, poor posture, smoking, high alcohol consumption, poor liver function.

17 COLDS, FLU AND FREQUENT INFECTIONS

Questionnaire

- Have you recently lost someone close to you?
- Are you recovering from surgery?
- Are you frequently under stress?
- Do you consume a lot of dairy produce?
- Are you suffering from any known food or environmental allergies?

Possible causes: lowered immune function, adrenal stress, food intolerances and gut permeability, bacterial infections, lack of vitamins A, C, E, zinc and selenium.

18 YEAST INFECTIONS AND CYSTITIS

Questionnaire

- Do you suffer from digestive problems?
- Do you frequently eat animal products?
- Is your diet high in sugar?
- Do you suffer from mouth ulcers (canker sores)?
- Are you urinating frequently?

Possible causes: gut dysbiosis and permeability, bacterial infections, high-acid diet.

19 EATING DISORDERS AND OBESITY

Questionnaire

- Are you afraid of food?
- Do you think about food all the time?
- Do you crave specific foods?
- Are you in the habit of weighing yourself daily?
- Are you more than 20 kilos (44 lb) overweight?
- Are you secretive about your eating habits?

Possible causes: imbalanced thyroid function, amino acid deficiencies, lack of zinc and vitamin B6, chromium and vitamin B3 deficiencies, too much or too little exercise, pancreatic insufficiency, poor blood-sugar management.

20 CONCENTRATION/MEMORY LOSS

Questionnaire

- Do you eat irregularly?
- Do you have a lot of amalgam tooth fillings?
- Are you a regular consumer of caffeinated drinks?
- Do you have food cravings?
- Are you suffering from any digestive discomfort?

Possible causes: toxic metals and environmental pollutants, bacterial and parasitic infections, poor blood-sugar management, multiple nutrient deficiencies.

your top 100 foods for health

Whatever your lifestyle, it's not difficult to make simple changes to your diet that will speedily improve your health. Forget your inclinations towards manufactured 'easy-to-prepare' foods – they're not so easy on your body as they are lacking in nutrition and often stuffed with potentially hazardous ingredients such as fat, sugar and salt. Our tasty selection is a rich larder of fabulous foods, chock-full of goodness: just look at what they can do for your body. They're not listed in any particular order, so read on and see how an army of highly trained defenders could soon be on your plate.

Food		Nutrients	Benefits
	Broccoli 1	Calcium, magnesium, phosphorus, vitamin B3, vitamin B5, beta-carotene, high in vitamin C and folic acid.	Anti-cancer, antioxidant, intestinal cleanser, excellent source of fibre, antibiotic, antiviral (from sulphur) – stimulates liver. A perfect food.
	Straw-berries 2	Vitamin A, vitamin C, vitamin K, beta-carotene, folic acid and potassium.	Anti-cancer, antiviral, antibacterial.
	Millet 3	Magnesium, potassium, phosphorus, vitamin B3.	Gluten-free grain, easily digestible. Highly alkaline. Rich in fibre. Low-allergenic food.
	Salmon 4	Calcium, selenium, vitamin D, vitamin E, omega-3 essential fatty acids.	Rich source of beneficial fish oil: good for hormonal health, skin, the immune system, bones and teeth.

Food	Nutrients	Benefits
Apple 5	Calcium, magnesium, phosphorus, vitamin C, beta-carotene, pectin.	Astringent, tonic. Relieves constipation, reactivates beneficial gut bacteria, reduces total cholesterol. Helps remove toxins.
Cabbage 6	Calcium, magnesium, potassium, phosphorus, beta-carotene, folic acid, vitamin C, vitamin E, vitamin K, iodine.	Eaten raw, it detoxifies the stomach and upper colon; improves digestion. Stimulates the immune system, kills bacteria and viruses. Anti-cancer and antioxidant. A perfect food.
Melon 7	Calcium, magnesium, potassium, phosphorus, vitamin C, beta-carotene.	Excellent cleanser and rehydrator. High water content. Should be eaten on its own for maximum benefit.
Pine nuts 8	Magnesium, potassium, zinc, B vitamins.	High in protein and essential fat. Good as a meat replacement for vegetarians.
Potatoes 9	Potassium, vitamin B3, folic acid, vitamin C.	Potato juice is very cleansing, benefiting the liver and muscles, and providing energy.
Orange 10	Calcium, potassium, beta-carotene, folic acid, vitamin C.	Stimulating, tonifying, cleansing. Internal antiseptic. Stimulates peristalsis.
Kidney beans 11	Calcium, magnesium, phosphorus, potassium, folic acid, protein.	High in fibre, cleanses the digestive tract. Increases beneficial bacteria, removes excess cholesterol.
Kiwi fruit 12	Magnesium, phosphorus, potassium, vitamin C.	Removes excess sodium in the body. An excellent source of digestive enzymes.

Food	Nutrients	Benefits
Chick peas 13	Calcium, magnesium, phosphorus, potassium, zinc, manganese, beta-carotene. High in folic acid. An excellent source of vegetable protein.	Support kidney function. Digestive cleanser.
Rice (brown) 14	Calcium, iron, magnesium, phosphorus, potassium, zinc, manganese, vitamin B3, vitamin B5, vitamin B6, folic acid.	Calming to the nervous system, relieves depression. An energy food. Rice water is beneficial for infant colic and alleviates diarrhoea.
Spinach 15	Beta-carotene, folic acid, potassium, iron, vitamin B6, vitamin C, calcium, magnesium.	Anti-cancer. Regulates blood pressure. Boosts the immune system. Supports bone health. A perfect food.
Avocado 16	Iron, copper, phosphorus, potassium, beta-carotene, folic acid, vitamin B3, vitamin B5, vitamin K. High in vitamin E.	Acid/alkaline content is balanced. Easily digested, good for the blood and prevents anaemia. A perfect food
Beetroot 17	Calcium, magnesium, iron, phosphorus, potassium, manganese, folic acid, vitamin C.	Excellent intestinal cleanser. Eliminates kidney stones. Good blood builder, detoxifies liver and gall bladder.
Oats 18	Calcium, magnesium, iron, phosphorus, manganese, vitamin B5, folic acid, silicon.	High fibre content ensures a mild laxative effect. Stimulate digestive function. Antioxidant properties. Excellent for bones and connective tissue.
Squash 19	Calcium, magnesium, phosphorus, potassium, beta-carotene, vitamin C.	Highly alkaline, relieves (marrow) acidosis of the liver and blood. Eating the seeds expels roundworms and tapeworms.
Tomato 20	Calcium, magnesium, phosphorus, beta-carotene, phosphorus, folic acid and vitamin C.	Contains over 90 per cent water. Antiseptic, alkaline. Raw tomatoes reduce liver inflammation. Eating large quantities can interfere with calcium absorption.

Food	Nutrients	Benefits
Tofu 21	Iron, amino acids, potassium, calcium, magnesium, vitamin A, vitamin K.	Perfect vegetarian source of protein. Balances hormones, anti-cancer, lowers cholesterol.
Asparagus 22	Phosphorus, potassium, folic acid, beta-carotene, vitamin C, vitamin K.	Contains asparagine, which stimulates the kidneys. Mild laxative, antibacterial. Caution: contains purine – avoid if you suffer from gout.
Nettles 23	Potassium, iron, vitamin C, beta-carotene.	Diuretic, detoxifying, anti-inflammatory. Nettle tea is good for gout and arthritis.
Rasp-berries 24	Calcium, magnesium, phosphorus, potassium, vitamin B3 and vitamin C.	Help expel mucus, phlegm, toxins. Excellent for female reproductive health. Raspberries relieve menstrual cramps. Raspberry-leaf tea reduces nausea in pregnancy.
Chicken 25	Vitamin A, vitamin B3, vitamin B6, vitamin K, sodium, potassium, magnesium.	Helps break up mucus during a cold. Mild antibiotic.
Herring 26	Omega-3 and omega-6 essential fatty acids, calcium, phosphorus.	Excellent blood cleanser, good for cardiovascular health.
Ginger 27	Calcium, magnesium, phosphorus, potassium.	Anti-spasmodic, prevents nausea, improves circulation. Good for menstrual cramps. Excellent for convalescence. A perfect food.
Bananas 28	Potassium, tryptophan, vitamin C, beta-carotene, vitamin K, vitamin B6.	Promote sleep. Mild laxative. Anti-fungal, natural antibiotic. Contain pectin, which helps ulcers, lowers cholesterol, and removes toxic metals from the body.

Food	Nutrients	Benefits
Rye 29	Calcium, iron, magnesium, phosphorus, potassium, zinc, manganese, vitamin E.	An energy food. Cleanses and renews arteries, benefits the liver, rebuilds the digestive system.
Soya beans 30	Calcium, iron, phosphorus, beta-carotene, amino acids, vitamin B3, vitamin C, omega-3 essential fatty acids, protein.	Contain all essential amino acids, making them a perfect vegetarian food. Soya is a potent phytoestrogen, which may help prevent breast and ovarian cancers. A primary source of lecithin, which controls cholesterol. A perfect food. Soya milk is a recommended alternative to cows' milk.
Walnuts 31	Calcium, iron, magnesium, phosphorus, zinc, potassium, folic acid, vitamin C, vitamin E.	Strengthen the kidneys and lungs, lubricate the digestive system, improve metabolism.
Apricots 32	Copper, calcium, magnesium, potassium, folic acid, vitamin C, beta-carotene, boron, iron.	Laxative, potent antioxidant, natural sweetener.
Watercress 33	Calcium, magnesium, phosphorus, potassium, vitamin C, beta-carotene.	Diuretic, breaks up kidney or bladder stones. One of the best foods for purifying the blood and relieving phlegm. High iodine content. Stimulates thyroid.
Psyllium seed 34	Calcium, magnesium, phosphorus, potassium, zinc.	Laxative, intestinal cleanser. Relieves autotoxaemia caused by constipation and bacterial/fungal infections.
Oysters 35	Very high in zinc. Vitamin A, vitamin B12, vitamin C, iron.	Benefit cardiovascular, immune and sexual function.
Quinoa 36	Calcium, iron, magnesium, phosphorus, potassium, vitamin B3.	Easy to digest. Gluten-free. Lysine content is a potent antiviral agent. Contains more calcium than milk. Stimulates milk flow in breastfeeding. Perfect vegetable protein.

Food	Nutrients	Benefits
Sea vegetables 37	Calcium, iron, potassium. Sea vegetables are seaweeds such as kelp,. carageen and samphire.	Highest source of these minerals, and excellent for cardiovascular and nervous systems. Cleanse the body of toxins, aid digestion. A perfect food for vegetarians.
Turnip 38	Calcium, magnesium, phosphorus, potassium, folic acid and vitamin C.	Eaten raw, turnip aids digestion, and cleans the teeth. Alkaline, so helps purify the body. May cause gas if digestion is weak. Helps clear the blood of toxins.
Pineapple 39	Calcium, magnesium, potassium, phosphorus, beta-carotene, vitamin C.	Contains bromelain, a potent digestive enzyme, scavenging bacteria and parasites: very similar to stomach acid. Not kind to tooth enamel.
Barley 40	Potassium, magnesium, phosphorus, calcium, zinc, manganese, B vitamins, folic acid.	Soothing to the digestive tract and liver, heals stomach ulcers, lowers cholesterol.
Artichoke 41	Calcium, magnesium, phosphorus, potassium, sodium, folic acid, beta-carotene, vitamin B3, vitamin C, vitamin K.	Diuretic, digestive. Contains inulin, which stimulates bacteria in the gut. Supports and cleanses the liver, promotes bile flow, lowers cholesterol.
Coconut 42	Magnesium, potassium, phosphorus, zinc, folic acid and vitamin C.	Regulates thyroid function.
Game (partridge, quail, pheasant, duck) 43	Selenium, full range of B vitamins, iron, zinc.	Energy-producing food: helps the body repair damage, and supports the immune system.
Mackerel 44	Calcium, selenium, vitamin E, omega-3 essential fatty acids.	Maintains cardiovascular health, balances hormones. Strengthens the immune system.

Food	Nutrients	Benefits
Papaya 45	Calcium, magnesium, potassium, vitamin C, beta-carotene.	Excellent for aiding digestion. Anti-parasitic, anti-cancer. Soothes intestinal inflammation and gas and detoxifies generally.
Tuna 46	Selenium, omega-3 essential fatty acids, vitamin B12, vitamin B3.	Good for the skin, hormonal and cardiovascular systems.
Almonds 47	Calcium, magnesium, phosphorus, potassium, zinc, folic acid, vitamin B2, vitamin B3, vitamin E.	Very alkaline, good source of protein, contain leatril (anti-cancer). Good building food for those who are underweight.
Brussel sprouts 48	Calcium, magnesium, iron, phosphorus, potassium, beta-carotene, vitamin B3, vitamin B6, vitamin C, vitamin E, folic acid.	Antioxidant, anti-cancer, antibacterial and antiviral. Support pancreatic function. Contain indoles, which protect against breast and colon cancer. Help guard against colon cancer (as does broccoli).
Cauliflower 49	Calcium, magnesium, folic acid, potassium, boron, beta-carotene, vitamin C.	Helps purify the blood. Good for bleeding gums, kidney and bladder disorders, high blood pressure, constipation. Anti-cancer and antioxidant.
Spirulina 50	Phosphorus, potassium, sodium, vitamin B3, gamma-linoleic acid, beta-carotene. Spirulina is a nutrient-rich algae available as a white powder. Can be added to soups and vegetable juices.	Easily digested, perfect protein. Benefits cell regeneration, reverses ageing, protects kidneys from the by-products of medicines. Fights tumours. Anti-fungal and antibacterial.
Sweet potato 51	Calcium, magnesium, potassium, folic acid, vitamin C, vitamin E, phosphorus, beta-carotene.	Easily digestible and highly nutritious. Excellent for inflammation of the digestive tract, ulcers and poor circulation. Detoxifying – binds to heavy metals and removes them from the body.
Radishes 52	Calcium, magnesium, potassium, phosphorus, beta-carotene, folic acid, vitamin C.	Expectorant, dissolve excess mucus or phlegm. Clear sinuses and sore throats. Aid production of digestive juices, particularly when eaten with starches.

Food	Nutrients	Benefits
Pear 53	Calcium, magnesium, phosphorus, potassium, beta-carotene, folic acid. High in iodine.	Diuretic, high iodine content. Beneficial for thyroid function. Contains pectin, which aids peristalsis and the removal of toxins.
Carrots 54	Calcium, magnesium, potassium, phosphorus, beta-carotene.	Superb detoxifier, excellent food for the health of the liver and digestive tract. Carrots help kidney function and kill bacteria and viruses.
Corn 55	Iron, magnesium, potassium, zinc, vitamin B3.	Excellent food for brain and nervous system. Good for eczema. Anti-cancer food. Rich source of essential fats.
Alfalfa 56	Calcium, magnesium, potassium, manganese, sodium.	Stimulant, reduces inflammation, detoxifies, encourages sexual activity. A perfect food – but contraindicated with lupus and other auto-immune diseases.
Prunes 57	Calcium, phosphorus, potassium, beta-carotene, iron acid.	Laxative, containing oxalic acid. Beneficial for blood, brain and nerves. Help to lower cholesterol.
Sesame seeds 58	Calcium, iron, magnesium, zinc, vitamin E, folic acid, phosphorus, potassium, copper, omega-3 and omega-6 essential fatty acids.	Strengthen heart and cardiovascular system and benefit nervous system. Contain lignans, which are antioxidant. Inhibit cholesterol absorption from the diet.
Blueberries 59	Vitamin C, beta-carotene.	Laxative, blood cleanser, improve circulation, benefit eyesight, antioxidant.
Celeriac 60	Calcium, magnesium, potassium, vitamin C.	Diuretic, good for stones and arthritis. Beneficial to the nervous and lymphatic systems.

Food	Nutrients	Benefits
Eggs 61	Calcium, iron, manganese, zinc, B-group vitamins. First-class protein.	Good for problems with the bones and joints, boost immune system
Figs 62	Calcium, phosphorus, potassium, beta-carotene, vitamin C.	Laxative, restorative, increase vitality. Move sluggish bowels, clear toxins. One of the highest plant sources of calcium.
Palm hearts 63	Beta-carotene, vitamin E.	Antibacterial, excellent for skin and hormonal health. Should be eaten in raw form (usually available in cans) and not cooked, because cooking releases toxins.
Parsley 64	Vitamin C, iron, calcium, sodium.	Cleanser, tonic, breath freshner. Alkaline. Cleanses blood, reduces coagulants in veins. Clears kidney stones.
Onion 65	Calcium, magnesium, phosphorus, potassium, beta-carotene, folic acid, quercetin	Antiseptic, anti-spasmodic, antibiotic. Reduces spasms in asthma. High capability for detoxifying – removes heavy metals and parasites.
Sunflower seeds 66	Vitamin A, vitamin B, vitamin D, vitamin E, vitamin K, calcium, iron, potassium, phosphorus, zinc, manganese, magnesium, omega-3 and omega-6 essential fatty acids.	A more beneficial nutrient source than most meats, eggs and cheese. Contain pectin, which removes toxins and heavy metals. Strengthen sight and sensitivity to light. A perfect food.
Buckwheat 67	Phosphorus, beta-carotene, vitamin C, calcium, magnesium, phosphorus, potassium, zinc, manganese, folic acid, essential amino acids. An excellent vegetable protein.	Strengthens capillaries, detoxifies. Contains all eight essential amino acids, making it good for the intestines. Not to be eaten by those with cancer or skin allergies.
Aubergine (Eggplant) 68	Calcium, phosphorus, beta-carotene, folic acid.	Cleans blood, prevents strokes and haemorrhages, protects arteries damaged by cholesterol.

Food	Nutrients	Benefits
Fennel 69	Calcium, magnesium, phosphorus, sodium, folic acid, vitamin C, potassium. Rich in phytoestrogens.	Anti-spasmodic, relieves intestinal cramps and stomach pain. Beneficial during the menopause. Digests fats well, useful in obesity and weight control.
Mango 70	High in beta-carotene, vitamin C.	Beneficial for kidneys, combats acidity and poor digestion. Good blood cleanser.
Lentils 71	Calcium, magnesium, phosphorus. Rich source of potassium, zinc and folic acid.	Good source of minerals for nearly every organ in the body. Neutralize acids produced in muscle.
Mush-rooms 72	Calcium, iron, magnesium. vitamin B3, vitamin B5, folic acid, zinc.	Thin the blood, lower cholesterol. Support immune function. Shiitake mushrooms contain a potent anti-cancer element.
Peas (dried/split) 73	Calcium, magnesium, phosphorus, B vitamins, folic acid, potassium, zinc, iron.	Good source of vegetable protein. Tone the stomach and aid liver function.
Olives 74	Calcium, iron, beta-carotene.	Easily digested. Beneficial for liver and gall bladder, increasing secretion of bile. Stimulate peristalsis.
Pepper 75	Potassium, beta-carotene, folic acid, vitamin B, vitamin C.	Antibacterial, stimulant. Normalizes blood pressure, improves circulatory system, boosts secretion of saliva and stomach acid, helps peristalsis.
Yam 76	Calcium, magnesium, phosphorus, vitamin C, potassium, folic acid.	Anti-arthritic, anti-spasmodic, diuretic, tonifying. Binds to heavy metals to aid detoxification. Excellent for symptoms of IBS, PMS and menopause. Regulates oestrogens.

Food	Nutrients	Benefits
Yoghurt 77	Calcium, vitamin D.	Beneficial to the intestinal tract by regenerating good bacteria. Soothing, cooling. Use live organic yoghurt only, which contains acidophilus bacteria.
Garlic 78	Calcium, phosphorus, potassium, vitamin C.	Anitbacterial, antiseptic, antiviral, decongestant. Lowers cholesterol. Nature's own anitbiotic. A perfect food.
Cashew nuts 79	Calcium, magnesium, iron, zinc, folic acid.	Improve vitality, good for teeth and gums.
Cherries 80	Calcium, phosphorus, vitamin C.	Antispasmodic, relieve headaches. Juice fights gout. Natural antiseptic.
Dates 81	Calcium, iron, beta-carotene, vitamin B3.	Excellent against diarrhoea and dysentry, good for problems with the respiratory system.
Leeks 82	Potassium, vitamin K, calcium, folic acid, vitamin A.	Cleansing, diuretic. Eliminate uric acid in gout.
Licorice 83	Magnesium, iron, calcium, phosphorus, manganese, vitamin B3, vitamin C.	Good for adrenal function. Diuretic, laxative. Cleanses mouth and teeth. May counteract some viruses such as herpes and HIV. Assists digestion and supports the liver.
Parsnip 84	Potassium, phosphorus, folic acid, calcium, magnesium.	Diuretic, supports kidneys and spleen. Detoxifies and cleanses the body. Improves bowel action.

Food	Nutrients	Benefits
Wild rice 85	Iodine, selenium, vitamin E, tryptophan (amino acid), potassium.	Excellent vegetarian source of protein.
Black-currants 86	Calcium, magnesium, potassium, phosphorus, beta-carotene, vitamin C.	Tonic and blood cleanser. Relieve diarrhoea.
Celery 87	Beta-carotene, folic acid, vitamin B3, sodium.	Contains coumarins, which have good anti-cancer properties. Lowers blood pressure, can help migraines. Aids digestion. Prevents fermentation. Helps arthritic joints, prevents calcium deposits.
Grapefruit 88	Calcium, magnesium, potassium, vitamin C.	Contains salicylic acid, which helps arthritis. Excellent for cardiovascular system. Blood cleansing. Good for allergies and infections of the throat and mouth.
Flaxseed (Linseed) 89	Omega-3 and omega-6 essential fatty acids, potassium, magnesium, calcium, phosphorus, iron, vitamin B3, vitamin E.	Alleviates constipation and bloating, helps eliminate toxic waste in bowels. Good for asthma. Strengthens the blood. Anti-inflammatory, anti-cancer. A perfect food.
Lemon/ Lime 90	Potassium, vitamin C.	Astringent, potent antiseptic, excellent for colds, coughs, sore throats. Dissolve gallstones. Anti-cancer properties.
Wheat 91	Calcium, iron, magnesium, phosphorus, potassium, zinc, manganese, vitamin B3, vitamin B5, vitamin B6, folic acid.	Organic wholewheat (unbleached, with no chemical washing, with germ and bran left intact) stimulates the liver and cleanses toxins.
Cucumber 92	Potassium, beta-carotene.	Diuretic, laxative. Dissolves the uric acid that causes kidney and bladder stones. Helps digestion. Regulates blood pressure.

Food	Nutrients	Benefits
Lettuce 93	Beta-carotene, magnesium, potassium, folic acid.	Anti-spasmodic. Contains silicon, which supports bones, joints, arteries and connective tissue.
Mung beans 94	Calcium, magnesium, iron, phosphorus, potassium, zinc, vitamin B3, vitamin B5, folic acid.	Great heart and blood cleanser, excellent for detoxification.
Peach 95	Calcium, magnesium, phosphorus, vitamin C, potassium, beta-carotene, folic acid.	Diuretic, laxative, easily digested, alkaline. Cleansing for kidneys and bladder.
Molasses 96	Calcium, magnesium, phosphorus, potassium, manganese, B vitamins.	Contains more calcium than milk. Use in moderation.
Okra 97	Calcium, magnesium, phosphorus, folic acid, vitamin B3, potassium, beta-carotene.	Soothing to the intestinal tract. Beneficial for IBS, bloating and gas.
Pumpkin seeds 98	Calcium, iron, magnesium, zinc, B vitamins, phosphorus, potassium, omega-3 essential fatty acids.	Excellent for prostate health. Remove intestinal parasites. Pumpkin seed oil is rich in omega-3 essential fatty acids (do not heat or the value is destroyed).
Cran-berries 99	Potassium, beta-carotene, vitamin C.	Excellent for the respiratory system. Kill bacteria and viruses in the kidneys, bladder and urinary tract.
Pepper-corns 100	Calcium, magnesium, potassium, manganese, phosphorus.	Digestive stimulant, antioxidant and antibacterial.

weight management

For many people, the decision to alter eating habits is often spurred on by a desire to lose weight. If this is your aim too, we can only say to you what we say to our clients: weight loss follows healthy eating. By making good health your goal, you are more likely to have a better understanding of food and with it a better knowledge of the factors affecting weight.

The diet industry feeds directly off the pressure applied by the fashion and beauty industries, which tell us that we must look good in order to feel good. Fortunes are spent advertising 'weight-loss' foods and diet drinks. While these can help some people, we believe that ultimately, dieting doesn't work. We have both come across clients who are truly unwell, yet who will not follow a new eating plan that is designed specifically to help them recover if it involves eating foods that they consider to be 'fattening'. These clients choose to stay unwell, rather than risk any weight gain.

Why diets don't work

Barely a week goes by without the introduction and promotion of some new fad diet – and while some weight loss will be experienced in the first few days, this is only due to the loss of fluid and not fat. Disappointment is inevitable.

We have seen many clients who have followed unsafe diets – diets driven by calories rather than nutrition – which result in actual health problems. For example, a high-protein diet, over a prolonged period, can lead to bone deterioration and kidney problems; a low-fat diet may interfere with hormonal health and brain function, affecting mood and self-perception.

Lose five pounds in five days?

Understanding what is actually lost, and what is not, is the key to safe and effective weight management. When we diet, we consume less food (fewer calories), causing the body to call upon its reserves to release glycogen, which is then used for energy. This glycogen, stored in the liver and lean muscle tissue, is held in a water base. The weight loss we experience in the early stages of a diet is simply a loss of fluid. This is the basis of the hollow promises behind diets that advertise themselves as a way of losing five pounds in five days. Yes, you do lose weight in terms of fluid loss, but there is no actual body fat loss, so the effect is temporary. If this approach is maintained for an extended period, the body perceives the relatively lower intake of food as potential starvation, so it holds on to whatever food or drink is consumed for fuel and glycogen replacement. This accounts for the dieting 'plateau' familiar to many habitual dieters who discover that, despite not eating very much, they still do not lose weight.

Yo-yo dieting – the thyroid disrupter

Yo-yo dieters are people who spend years trying one diet after another. They are imprisoned in an eternal treadmill of losing weight, gaining weight, losing it again and, inevitably, gaining more. The frustration that this causes them is enormous, frequently bringing with it problems of depression, low self-esteem and even hormonal disruption.

The speed at which we burn up our food to convert it into energy (our metabolic rate) is governed by the thyroid gland, located at the base of the throat. This gland is essential for energy production, dictating how we feel on a day-to-day basis. Yo-yo dieting confuses the delicate balance of hormones that are fed to and from the thyroid, resulting in a slower metabolic rate. The result of this more sluggish metabolic rate is that the thyroid slows down and resets the storage levels of glycogen in the body – holding on to it rather than releasing it – making weight loss impossible.

Stress

Two hormones released in times of stress are cortisol and DHEA (see page 58). Stress alters the balance of the hormones and can encourage fat storage even when food intake is restricted. The dieter cannot lose weight, and dieting itself becomes a stress factor.

Allergies and intolerances

Sometimes we develop an intolerance towards foods that we eat every day. When an intolerance has developed, the body will hold on to fluids to protect any potentially vulnerable areas, such as the intestinal tract. This water retention causes puffiness and weight gain.

If someone is intolerant to wheat, merely eating a bowl of cereal and a piece of toast in the morning, a salad sandwich for lunch, a mid-afternoon biscuit, and pasta with fresh tomato sauce in the evening, will almost guarantee weight gain, because over 50 per cent of the day's food has contained wheat. We have found that by cutting wheat out of their diet, our clients have experienced increased energy levels, decreased tissue puffiness and a reduction in weight. If you suspect a food intolerance, keep a food diary (see page 32) – it will highlight how frequently you are consuming the same foods.

Blood-sugar imbalance

We have found that virtually everyone who finds it difficult to lose weight has a marked blood sugar imbalance. Resolving this hormonal imbalance is the first step to true fat loss. It also has the added bonus of reducing inflammation, improving mood, concentration and energy levels and eliminating food cravings. There is no substitute for fresh, colourful fruit and vegetables. The nutrients they contain support the thyroid gland and maintain a healthy metabolic rate, while their fibre content helps to remove excess fats from the body. It is best to eat fruit and vegetables raw, since cooking can destroy fibre and nutrients.

Surprisingly, we need fats to help maintain healthy weight levels. The essential fatty acids found in nuts, seeds, oily fish and olive oil are all vital for the movement of stored fats out of the adipose tissues, and important to weight management. All cells in the body have a fatty layer that protects them from potential damage,

as well as allowing nutrients in, and waste matter and toxins out. This fatty layer is made up from essential fatty acids, which cannot be manufactured in the body and must be derived from the diet. If the intake of essential fatty acids is inadequate, the cell walls become more rigid, preventing toxins, such as stored fats, from leaving. The fat becomes denser and more difficult to shift as time goes on. So to get rid of fat and cellulite, eat essential fatty acids. For this reason, oily fish such as sardines, mackerel, herring, tuna and salmon, which are rich in essential fatty acids, should be major protein sources for anyone following a weight management programme. For vegetarians, good sources of essential fatty acids are seeds, such as

Making the right choices – a good daily menu
Forget your preconceptions and refer to the chart below to see how a typical day's meals can be balanced, varied and delicious! These are just a few examples from the recommendations we make to our clients. (See pages 130–155 for recipes.)

breakfast

A glass of fresh fruit or vegetable juice, together with any one of the following:
- tofu smoothie
- millet porridge
- natural organic bio yoghurt with fruit of choice plus ground seeds such as pumpkin, sesame or sunflower
- sugar-free cornflakes or muesli (granola) with rice milk
- scrambled or poached eggs with tomatoes and mushrooms

mid-morning snack

Choose one of the following:
- apple or pear with cottage cheese
- palmful of pumpkin seeds, almonds or walnuts
- half an avocado
- organic blue corn chips and houmous

lunch

- Vegetable soup and a large leafy salad plus four raw vegetables from this list.

broccoli, shredded cabbage, grated carrots or pumpkin, raw beetroot, mushrooms, spring (green) onions, radishes, cauliflower, peas, sweetcorn

Together with either:
- cottage cheese
- a piece of lean chicken breast (no skin)
- a can of tuna fish, sardines or salmon

Or:
- grilled fish with steamed vegetables

Plus:
- some fruit, such as a banana, apple, a few berries, tinned cherries (syrup or sugar-free)

linseeds, pumpkin, sunflower and sesame, and cold-pressed oils made from them. Olive oil may also be used in moderation.

As well as diet, regular exercise has many benefits for the body, and helps to maintain a healthy balance of blood-sugar levels. Resolving to

carried out all over the body on a daily basis, to stimulate lymphatic drainage, and help to break down the stored fatty deposits. Use a natural bristle brush, rather than one that has been manufactured from synthetic fibres, and brush the skin in sweeping strokes toward the centre of the body.

Surprisingly, we need fats to help maintain healthy weight levels. Essential fatty acids are the good guys, helping to move stored fats out of adipose tissues.

increase exercise levels can be difficult when many of us tend to lead sedentary lives. For some, sustaining impetus may involve joining a gym for workouts and exercise classes; for others, taking a daily walk or walking to work three days a week is more easily achieved. Don't procrastinate – make the commitment to yourself today and make sure you follow it through.
To aid weight loss, skin brushing should be

The healthy eating chart below is an example of how you can arrange your daily diet to balance your blood-sugar levels, increase your vitality and promote all-round good health, while also addressing weight management. Follow the principle of combining some protein with carbohydrate at each meal, to ensure maintenance of blood-sugar levels and to prevent the possibility of food cravings.

mid-afternoon snack

Choose one of the following:

- a piece of fruit such as an orange, small bunch of grapes or a plum
- palmful of mixed nuts and seeds
- two oatcakes with tahini, guacamole or avocado dip

dinner

A serving of a primary protein, such as:

- fish, turkey or chicken with at least three vegetables and brown or wild rice
- rice or noodles with stir-fried chicken
- tofu and mixed vegetable stir-fry, including red peppers, carrots, french beans, mangetout (sugar snap peas), ginger, onions, mushrooms

bedtime snack

Choose one of the following:

- cottage cheese and two oatcakes
- a banana
- rice cake with houmous or nut spread (unsalted and sugar-free)

food allergies

Allergic reactions are now quite common. Many more of us experience allergies than people did fifty years ago. This rise can be attributed to the increase in environmental pollution, the use of pesticides and the abundance of other chemicals we use or are exposed to in our everyday lives. It is estimated that we are subjected to approximately 3,000 different chemicals every year – so it is no wonder that allergies are on the increase.

Every day, our immune systems are challenged by the chemicals we ingest in food and drinks, and the potentially toxic substances we inhale. This constant battle causes the liver to become overloaded, consequently making allergic reactions more prevalent.

In Britain, the most common food allergens are wheat, dairy products, citrus fruits and eggs. In terms of human evolution, wheat is a relatively new food, having only been farmed for the last 10,000 years. It is not clear whether wheat intolerance is due to man's lack of adaptation to the grain, or if the pesticides, herbicides and chemical processes involved in preparing the grains are behind it. Wheat-based foods often form the major part of the Western daily diet, so it is possible that lack of variety may be the cause of the problem.

Gluten allergy is a more severe form of grain allergy, and is brought on by oats, wheat, rye and barley. Those who suffer from coeliac disease (see Digestive Conditions, page 74) are unable to tolerate any of these grains. In severe cases, gluten allergy can become life-threatening as the gluten erodes the delicate lining of the digestive tract and prevents the absorption of the essential nutrients.

When is an allergy not an allergy?

There is some confusion about allergies and intolerances. While their effects are similar, their causes are different. An allergy is defined as an immediate reaction to any stimulus, causing the immune system to produce antibodies to attack the offending molecule.

An intolerance is a delayed reaction (often not manifesting itself for several days) that causes a wide variety of symptoms, often seemingly unrelated. The chart on page 31 illustrates these differences.

In addition, many symptoms are not obviously connected to food intolerance. The range of reactions is so wide that they are often attributed to causes other than food intolerance. Such symptoms include depression, joint pain, swollen eyes, sallow, pale and/or dry skin, 'brain

Allergy or intolerance?

There are subtle differences between a food allergy and a food intolerance. The body's reactions to a suspect food helps to determine a diagnosis. To ascertain if you have an allergy or an intolerance, check the chart below.

	allergy	intolerance
reaction time	immediate	delayed
causes	histamine and antibodies	antibodies
symptoms	hives (urticaria), rash, swelling, vomiting, palpitations, blushing, sudden tiredness	itching, raised pulse, fatigue, water retention, muscle soreness, dark circles under the eyes, headaches and migraines

fog' (difficulty in concentrating and thinking clearly), shallow breathing, constipation and/or diarrhoea, mouth ulcers (canker sores), runny nose, indigestion, skin rashes, bags and/or shadows under eyes and bed-wetting in children.

The genetic factor

Although it is common to find allergies in children of parents who have a history of allergic problems, it does not always follow that every such child will be susceptible. The evidence indicates that children of parents who have had asthma, eczema or hayfever (atopic allergies) will have an increased susceptibility, particularly if both parents are sufferers. The fault seems to lie in the genes that determine the suppression of the release of IgE, a chemical substance in the body which is one of the mediators of the acute, instant inflammatory response to specific allergens. However, genes are not the only cause of allergy. For example, identical twins do not necessarily develop the same allergies, which indicates that other external factors, such as environmental, bacterial or viral components, may also play a part in an an individual's likelihood of developing allergies.

Digestion and allergies

Approximately 70 per cent of the body's immune system lies in the digestive tract, making this area highly reactive to troublesome foods and substances. The most disruptive problem for the intestines is when an overgrowth of *Candida albicans* occurs.

nutrition know-how

If you always have a sandwich for lunch, ensure that the type of bread and its fillings are rotated daily to prevent intolerances brought on by a repetitive diet. Try rye, wholegrain or ciabatta bread with a chicken, tuna, cheese or salad filling.

Although *Candida* is an organism that is normally found in the gut, when the immune system is compromised, *Candida* may get out of control and become a problem. When this happens, the candida becomes invasive, burrowing its way through the intestinal wall and creating holes and spaces in an otherwise well-guarded barrier wall. The holes and spaces allow food particles, which would not normally pass into the bloodstream, to cause immune responses there. This is a typical cause of headaches and food intolerance-related migraines.

Dealing with allergies and intolerances

A healthy digestive tract and an efficient immune system are essential for alleviating or preventing allergies and intolerances. Identifying trigger foods and other substances is the first step to tackling the problem. Therefore, working closely with a nutrition consultant is one of the most productive ways of approaching the subject of food allergies.

Symptomatic problems in children can often be rapidly relieved by eliminating certain trigger foods. For example, in cases of hyperactivity or attention deficit hyperactivity disorder (ADHD), the simple removal of foods that include additives and colourings often has immediate positive effects.

In adults, many long-term health problems, not previously associated with food interactions, can often be banished permanently by following exclusion programmes devised with a nutrition consultant. Eating foods in season and rotating foods daily can also help eliminate many minor food intolerances.

Allergy testing

Many foods irritate both the digestive tract and the body as a whole. There are a variety of different types of test that can be carried out to determine allergies, ranging from a skin-prick test, to a full blood test to measure the antibody reaction caused by individual foods. The results of these tests are not always conclusive, since false positives as well as false negatives often appear. Many clients come to us with lengthy lists of foods they cannot eat. Upon further examination and investigation, we often discover that they have a compromised digestive tract function, which is causing the numerous food intolerances. To overcome this, we address the health of the digestive tract, in particular the integrity of the gut wall, and advise measures to promote its well-being. These measures usually overcome many of the food intolerance reactions, allowing our clients to enjoy their favourite foods again.

Food diaries

In our experience, keeping a food diary that details all your food and liquid intake, and subsequent reactions, is a very accurate method of pinpointing those foods that are causing problems. You can also keep a record of your emotional reactions to foods. For example, some people may find that within 24 hours of eating

Anaphylactic shock

For some people, a single food could prove life-threatening if they are allergic to it and the reaction is not spotted immediately and treated appropriately. Such extreme reactions are likely to occur within minutes of consuming a food and can be recognized by the symptoms opposite.

- Closing up of the throat and nasal passages

- Inability to breathe

- Anxiety

- Panic attack

- Acute swelling of any part, or all of the face and neck

tomatoes they experience joint pain, water retention and irritability; others may be vulnerable to bread and pasta, suffering reactions such as depression, headaches or sneezing.

However, if you suspect a food intolerance, it is advisable to let a qualified nutrition consultant or allergy specialist decipher your food diary. If delayed reactions are prevalent, intolerances may not be easy to determine.

Anaphylactic shock

Anaphylactic shock is an extreme, dangerous and possibly life-threatening reaction to an antigen. Peanuts are well known for their potential to cause anaphylactic shock: many food products now carry warnings that they contain peanuts or other nuts, which may cause an allergic reaction in susceptible people. Shellfish is another major culprit behind this type of reaction, although no warning labels currently appear on such foods. Bee and wasp stings may also cause anaphylactic shock. If anaphylactic shock occurs, take the patient to hospital immediately as they may need an adrenalin (epinephrine) injection. Check with the patient, as some sufferers carry their own injection with them. If swelling is severe, put a straw in his or her mouth to help aid breathing

Total toxic overload

There are those who find that they have become apparently intolerant to 'almost everything'. This is usually due to a severe gut dysbiosis, where the intestinal tract has become so inflamed that rogue food particles can pass through into the bloodstream unchecked. It is vital to address the digestive problems first, and allow the inflammation to settle.

It is also possible that the liver has become overburdened if a high intake of sugar, alcohol or prescription drugs has been consumed over a prolonged period. If the liver is overtaxed, many food intolerance-type symptoms will present themselves, and it is essential to follow a liver support programme. Consult a nutritionist for a personal programme.

cooking methods

Cookery is both an art form and a pleasure. If it is done well, the look and flavour of many foods is enhanced. However, as soon as the food is subjected to heat, its nutrient level can diminish. While we recommend eating (where it is safe to do so) as many raw foods as possible, we know that this does not suit everyone. We need to establish a balance between flavour and nutrient value.

Cooking changes the internal make-up of foods, making them more digestible and available for use by the body. In some cases however, cooking can damage food to such an extent that it is turned into a potential carcinogen. For example, frying oils alters their chemical structure, rendering them harmful to vulnerable body tissue such as the cardiovascular system (see Heart and Circulation, page 104).

Some methods of cooking and preparing foods are better than others for preserving the nutrient and water levels of food. Vitamin C and all the B group of vitamins are water-soluble, and can easily evaporate during intense cooking.

Steaming

Steaming foods is perhaps the most efficient way of preserving their nutrient content. Bring a little water to the boil and place the food (usually vegetables or fish) in a steamer above the bubbling water. The steam will cook the food in just a few minutes. Dense vegetables such as carrots and broccoli usually take five minutes or so, while leaves such as spinach take less than a minute to cook. The vegetables are left *al dente* (an Italian expression, meaning they remain firm) after steaming, retaining their vivid colours, fibrous structure and nutrient content.

Steaming fish usually takes about ten minutes and preserves the delicate 'good' fats that most fish contains, as well as the water-soluble B vitamins. Fish can be steamed over water flavoured with ginger, lemon juice or fragrant herbs – an excellent way to enhance its flavour.

Boiling

Boiling foods, especially vegetables, is the best way of making them dull and lifeless, with little nutrient content. It has been said that if vegetables such as carrots are boiled for ten minutes, the water contains more vitamin C than the carrots. Indeed, it would be better to drink the water and throw out the carrots!

As a rule of thumb, remember that boiling vegetables destroys approximately 40 per cent of B vitamins and 70 per cent of vitamin C. The greater the amount of water in the pan, the greater the nutrient loss. This loss is further heightened when the vegetables are cut into small pieces, as a greater surface area is exposed to the water and the heat, and this can further diminish nutrient levels.

In many countries, it is common to add salt to the water when boiling vegetables. This is unnecessary: most people's diets are already too high in salt. Salt upsets the body's own sodium/water balance, as well as the heart muscle's natural rhythm. All fruit and vegetables naturally contain some sodium, and it is usually

the extreme heat depletes the nutrients and disturbs the sensitive oils contained in foods such as oily fish and poultry. Cooking oils all have what is known as a 'smoke point': the temperature at which the oil burns. Each oil has a different smoke point – extra-virgin olive oil burns at the highest temperature.

Frying food creates abundant free radicals. Free radicals are atoms that damage the body – they are involved in the initiation of cancer, in heart

Both deep and shallow frying produce foods that are palatable and attractive, yet potentially damaging.

only palates that have been numbed by excessive stimulants, alcohol and sugars that crave added salt. (See page 109 for more information on salt and the heart.) So, if you are boiling food, do so for the minimum length of time, using only a small quantity of water, to preserve maximum nutrient content. Better still, steam it instead.

Frying

Both deep and shallow frying produce foods that are palatable and attractive, yet potentially damaging. Although the food is cooked quickly,

disease (see arteriosclerosis and atherosclerosis, page 110) and premature ageing. Free radicals can be countered by eating foods rich in antioxidants (see the Fighting Five, page 116). However, antioxidants are easily damaged by the high temperatures involved in frying. Browning foods by frying them, or worse still, letting them burn a little, is known to be carcinogenic. Even the smoke from frying foods can be dangerous – cooks who fry food on a frequent basis have a higher risk of lung and throat cancer than those who do not.

Vitamins that are soluble in water (B and C) and fat (D, A, K and E) are lost during shallow and deep frying. Frying meat or poultry decreases its vitamin B content by as much as 30 per cent.

Stir-frying

While stir-frying foods in a wok is always seen as the healthy alternative to deep or shallow frying, it is nonetheless still frying. Nutrients may be lost and fats are chemically altered.

However, the quantity of oil used is minimal in comparison, and the food cooks fast, because the wok ensures an even distribution of heat. If the food is cooked quickly and moved around all the time, damage is minimized.

Try adding a tablespoon of water and one of soy sauce to the oil as it heats. The liquid will stop the oil from burning, and as it evaporates it will provide some steam to help cook the food. Best of all, part-cook the food in advance (steaming is best) and use the wok to 'finish' the food.

Microwaving

Microwaving food causes the water molecules in it to move, and this movement creates the heat which cooks the food. The microwaves bounce off the oven walls and into the food. Nutrient levels of vegetables remain reasonably high after microwaving, probably due to the short cooking time – which is the main advantage of this cooking method. However, nutrients are still

lost, so steaming vegetables is a preferable method of cooking.

One of the biggest problems with this cooking method is the type of food that is generally cooked in microwave ovens. Processed 'ready meals', which can be microwaved in a few minutes, contain sugar, salt and often hydrogenated fats – all of which can be harmful to the body. In addition, when they are microwaved, these foodstuffs are the most susceptible to certain molecular changes. This change in the molecular structure can lead to free radical damage.

Stewing and soup-making

Cooking by stewing utilizes an extended simmering process. Stewing foods, or making casseroles and soups, ensures that the cooking liquid is served and eaten as well as the original food, so we benefit from the nutrients that are transferred into the water.

The advantage of stewed foods is that they are cooked slowly, usually at temperatures below boiling point. As vitamin and mineral loss increases with temperature, this method does not disturb the nutrient level greatly. Stewing also makes protein foods more digestible, as the fibres in the food are broken down, rendering them easier for us to absorb.

Some fruits actually benefit from stewing. For example, the enzymes in prunes are freed during this slow and gentle cooking method. Stewing fruits intensifies the taste of the natural sugar content so the flavour is best balanced with a little unsweetened live bio yoghurt.

Roasting

Roasting meats, poultry and vegetables is a popular way to prepare foods and is an age-old cooking method in the West. The fat content of the food is relatively undisturbed, as long as the oven isn't too hot. However, if fats are allowed to burn, they become potentially carcinogenic. The browning that is synonymous with roasting is due to carbohydrates, in the form of sugars, reacting to the heat.

Some water-soluble vitamins, such as vitamin C and B-complex vitamins, are inevitably lost during roasting. It is estimated that approximately 25 per cent of B vitamins are lost during roasting, although the longer the food is cooked, the greater the vitamin loss. The same is true of temperature – the higher the temperature, the greater the nutrient loss.

Barbecuing

A summer barbecue is always popular. The foods that are traditionally cooked on barbecues are the protein foods meat and fish. Many people prefer to eat them slightly burnt on the outside. However, burnt food has the potential to be carcinogenic – when it comes into direct contact with the throat and digestive tract, it damages cells, leading to an increase in harmful free radicals.

To minimize damage from barbecued foods, ensure that the barbecue is hot – the coals should be white-hot and glowing, with no flames. Avoid using firelighters – foods cooked directly in their flame may become coated with the chemicals contained in the firelighters. Because of the intense heat that the food is subjected to, barbecued foods all too often appear cooked on the outside but are found to be raw in the centre. For this reason it is advisable to part-cook food in the oven first, then use the barbecue to finish the process.

Raw food

This is by far the best way to benefit from all the available nutrients. We are not suggesting that you eat meat or grains raw, simply that you eat some raw vegetables, fruit, nuts or seeds every day. The benefit of raw foods is that they contain their own digestive enzymes, which lessen the demand on the pancreas to produce these enzymes. They are also abundant sources of fibre, which encourages the removal of toxic waste and excess cholesterol from the body.

If your food usually comes with the instructions to 'pierce film several times', we encourage you to set aside a little more time for cooking and eating, whenever possible. Turn to page 130 to find some suggestions for healthy, nutritious meals. Most of our recipes are quick, simple and require minimal fuss, proving that good food can be prepared in minutes – but with positive effects that last a lifetime.

nutrition know-how

Marinating barbecue food in olive oil (which is rich in vitamin E) before cooking, offers some protection against damage by the free radicals let loose by the barbecue process.

part one

Energy
and Emotions

good food, good mood

The food we eat is used to make the energy required for every function in the body – from walking and talking, to digesting and breathing. But why do we often complain of a lack of energy, or of feeling irritable and listless? The answer lies in the type of foods that make up our daily diet.

Energy boosting

As well as water and air, we require a constant, regular intake of food to provide the major source of energy for movement, breathing, heat regulation, heart function, blood circulation and brainpower. It is staggering to realize that, even at rest, our brain uses approximately 50 per cent of the energy that is derived from the food we consume, and considerably more than that when we actively engage our minds, such as in a period of intense work or when sitting an exam. So how is the food transformed into energy?

The process of digestion, which is described more fully in the digestion section (pages 69-79), breaks down all foods into single molecules of glucose, which are then transported through the gut wall into the bloodstream. The glucose is carried to the liver, where it is filtered and stored ready for use. The pituitary gland in the brain directs a series of hormonal releases from the pancreas and adrenal glands, which stimulate the liver to release the stores of glucose back into the bloodstream to be delivered to whichever organs and muscles require it.

Once it reaches its target organ, the glucose enters individual cells where it is converted into an energy source that the cell can use. The process of keeping the organs supplied with energy is known as blood-sugar management.

To maximize our energy, we need to include certain foods in our diets, especially those that boost the metabolism and those that sustain consistent energy levels. To understand how these foods benefit us, we need to consider the following factors:

How does food become energy?

Every cell contains several mitochondria. Here, the constituent parts of food undergo a series of chemical reactions, producing energy. In this way, each cell acts like a tiny power plant. It is interesting to note that the number of mitochondria we have in each of our cells is dependent upon our energy needs. If we exercise regularly, the number of mitochondria increases to meet the demand for higher energy production. Conversely, leading a sedentary lifestyle will lead to a decrease of energy output

LEFT Cabbage contains the minerals required for concentration and good moods.

efficiency, and a correspondingly lower number of mitochondria. These chemical reactions require the presence of a large number of nutrients, each of which is specific to different parts of the process of energy production (see Energy foods, page 45). Apart from the importance of an individual food's nutrient content, it is also vital to eat certain types of food in order to obtain energy: carbohydrates, protein and fat.

flight' response (see page 43), glycogen is released into the bloodstream to make extra energy available for the body. The glycogen is held in a water base.

Protein balanced with carbohydrates

While everyone's diet should contain a mix of carbohydrates and protein, each individual has a personal level at which the two are optimally balanced, depending on lifestyle. Achieving your

It is important to minimize those dietary factors that rob the body of energy or interfere with energy production. All such foods stimulate the hormone adrenaline.

It is important to keep blood glucose at an even level for concentration and alertness (see Blood-sugar management, pages 44-46). Eating foods that have a low glycaemic value will help to maintain blood sugar levels. Adding some protein and fibre to every meal or snack will help to sustain consistent energy levels throughout the day.

Carbohydrates and glucose

The energy that we derive from food is more likely to come from carbohydrates than from protein or fat. Carbohydrates are more easily converted into glucose, and are therefore the most convenient food for the body to use to manufacture energy.

The glucose can be turned into immediate energy, and any excess is kept as a reserve in the liver and the muscles. It is stored in the form of glycogen, which is easily converted back into glucose when required. During the 'fight or

personal balance can only be done through trial and error, but the quantities on the table opposite provide a guideline.

Take care with your protein intake. Always match protein with high-quality complex carbohydrates such as dense vegetables or wholegrains. Eating too much protein stimulates the body into an acid state, while it should be slightly alkaline. The body's built-in buffering systems work to change an acid state to an alkaline one, by releasing calcium from the bones. Eventually this can compromise bone

nutrition know-how

Glucose drinks and snack bars provide an instant energy rush, but it is short-lived. This further depletes the body's energy stores. During exercise you use up lots of energy so, for a pre-exercise drink, try a tofu smoothie with fresh berries and vanilla rice-milk.

Your lifestyle	What you need (ratio of protein to carbohydrate)
INACTIVE **Elderly, sedentary,** **recuperating**	**protein 1 : $3/4$ carbohydrate**
MORE ACTIVE **Office worker, shopkeeper,** **homemaker**	**protein 1 : $2/3$ carbohydrate**
ACTIVE LIFESTYLE **Exercising regularly, working** **mother, student**	**protein 1 : 2 carbohydrate**
MOST ACTIVE **Athlete or bodybuilder,** **tradesperson**	**protein 1 : $1/2$ – 2 carbohydrate**

health, leading to the bone-thinning disease osteoporosis, in which fractures readily occur.

Experiment by increasing your protein intake a little and decreasing your carbohydrates, or vice versa, until you feel your energy levels are higher and remain consistent.

Energy requirements during life

At various times during our lives we need extra energy. For example, in childhood we need energy for growth and learning, while during adolescence it is also required for the hormonal and physical changes that take place in the body during puberty. During pregnancy, both mother and baby place extra demands on energy supplies, and throughout our lives we use up extra energy during periods of stress. In addition, if you have an active life and/or a non-sedentary job, you will need more energy than those who do not.

Energy stealers

It is important to minimize those dietary factors that rob the body of energy or interfere with energy production. These include alcohol, tea, coffee and fizzy drinks, as well as cakes, biscuits and sweets. All such foods stimulate the hormone adrenaline, which is made by the adrenal glands. Adrenaline is produced primarily when the body perceives a threat or a challenge – the 'fight or flight' syndrome – to prepare itself for action. It causes the heart to beat faster, the lungs to take in more air, the liver to release extra glucose into the blood, and blood to divert from non-vital areas to where it will be of more use, such as the legs. If adrenaline is constantly over-produced because of stimulant foods, it may lead to general fatigue.

Stress is also an energy stealer, because it encourages the release of stored glucose from the liver and muscles, providing short-term

43

energy but long-term fatigue, as energy stores are constantly being depleted. During the 'fight or flight' response, the liver releases glycogen (stored sugars) into the blood, raising blood sugar. Therefore prolonged exposure to stress can play havoc with blood sugar levels. In the same way, caffeine and stimulants such as nicotine in cigarettes also raise blood sugar by stressing the adrenal glands – these release two hormones, cortisol and adrenaline, which interfere with the digestive process and direct the liver to release stored glycogen.

Energy foods

The most important energy foods are those rich in the B-complex group of vitamins, which comprises vitamins B1, B2, B3, B5, B6, B12, B9 (folic acid) and biotin. They are all found in abundance in the wholegrains of millet, buckwheat, rye, quinoa (a South American grain that is becoming more widely available), corn and barley. If these grains are sprouted, their energy quotient is increased many times, as the enzyme action involved in the sprouting process increases the nutrient value. The range of B-complex vitamins is also to be found in fresh green vegetables.

Other nutrients that are required for energy production are vitamin C, found in fruit and vegetables such as oranges, potatoes and peppers; magnesium, which is found in green vegetables, nuts and seeds; zinc, from egg yolks, fish and sunflower seeds; iron, plentiful in grains, pumpkin seeds and lentils; copper, part of the make-up of brazil nuts, oats, salmon and mushrooms; and co-enzyme Q10, found in beef, sardines, spinach and peanuts.

Blood-sugar management

How many times have you woken up feeling groggy, bad-tempered and in need of another couple of hours' sleep? You don't feel equipped to start the day. Or perhaps, having reached mid-morning, you wonder how you will manage to continue until your lunch break. Worse still, how often do you feel exhausted by mid-afternoon, knowing that you have several more hours of work to do, the journey home to cope with, and then dinner to cook and eat? Do you ask yourself, 'Whatever happened to all that energy I used to have?'

Constant fatigue and lack of energy can have many different causes but, quite often, they are the result of a poor and/or irregular diet, and the increasing consumption of stimulants to 'keep going' throughout the day.

Depression, irritability and mood swings, as well as premenstrual tension, outbursts of anger, anxiety and nervousness can all be the result of imbalances in energy production, nutrient deficiencies and frequent fad dieting.

Understanding the basics of energy production in the body shows us how we can, within a remarkably short time, ensure a higher and more constant level of energy all day long – and still have enough stamina to enjoy the latter part of the day, as well as experiencing more restorative sleep during the night.

Glucose, not sugar

The molecules broken down from protein, fats and carbohydrates are complex sugars, unlike the sugar that is added to commercial cereals

Energy foods – as simple as ABC

There are three different grades of energy food – A, B and C. The A-grade foods are the most effective. The B-grade foods also provide good levels of energy, but not quite as much as the A-foods. C-grade foods provide 'cheap' energy – you get a quick energy surge, but it is not lasting. At times when extra energy is required, try to eat lots of small meals throughout the day, which include A- or B-grade carbohydrates and protein.

A-grade foods

- **Complex carbohydrates**
  Wholegrains such as oats, barley, brown rice, millet, wholegrain bread, rye bread, corn bread
- **Vegetables**
  Dense vegetables such as broccoli, cauliflower, brussels sprouts, mushrooms, turnips, carrots (especially raw), asparagus, artichokes, spinach
- **Fruit**
  Avocado, apple, pear, pineapple, berries – strawberries, raspberries, blackberries, cherries
- **Protein**
  Salmon, tuna, herring, mackerel, seaweeds, eggs, tofu, walnuts, brazil nuts, sunflower seeds, pumpkin seeds, sesame seeds, linseeds. Sprouted seeds and grains, haricot and lima beans, chick peas, lentils and soya beans

B-grade foods

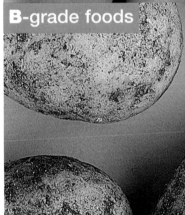

- **Complex carbohydrates**
  Buckwheat, red macrobiotic rice, wild rice, oatcakes
- **Vegetables**
  Potato, sweet potato, corn, squash, beetroot, peppers, wild rice, yam, watercress, salad leaves
- **Fruit**
  Peach, apricot, mango, papaya, banana
- **Protein**
  Kidney beans, black beans, peas (dried/split), almonds, chicken, game, turkey, venison, nut butters, yoghurt, cottage cheese, fish

C-grade foods

- **Simple carbohydrates**
  White pasta, bread, rice, rice noodles, egg noodles
- **Vegetables**
  Tomato, green peas, zucchini, cucumber
- **Fruit**
  Prunes, all dried fruit, grapes, figs
- **Protein**
  Dairy products such as cheese and milk, red meats, duck, veal

(granolas), fizzy drinks, cakes and biscuits. Carbohydrates are the best source of fuel for the body, as they can be most easily converted into glucose. However, a diet that is too high in carbohydrates can upset the delicate balance of blood sugar levels, causing them to fluctuate wildly. It is best to balance all carbohydrates with fibre, protein and a little fat.

When food is digested and absorbed into the bloodstream, hormones trigger the pancreas to release insulin to help transport glucose across the individual cell membranes. If the level of sugar (glucose) in the bloodstream is in excess of what the body requires, the surplus is sent to the liver to be stored until needed.

However, if the blood sugar level rises too rapidly, the pancreas responds by releasing a large dose of insulin. This causes the highs and lows that many people experience after eating a sweet snack. A bar of chocolate may be a great 'pick-me-up', giving a quick fix of energy, but within a short space of time the eater will feel more lethargic than he or she did to start with. This pancreatic reaction is known as 'reactive hypoglycaemia'. Over an extended period, it can lead to mature-onset diabetes, unless changes are made to the diet. The production and release of insulin from

nutrition know-how

Drinking tea or coffee for a quick boost creates unnecessary stress on the body and provides only short-lived energy. Replace with green tea, which is low in caffeine and high in antioxidant action, or diluted orange juice.

the pancreas is initiated by vitamin B3 (niacin) and the mineral chromium, which work together. Chromium is frequently found to be deficient in those who suffer from reactive hypoglycaemia and those with poor diets, as the pancreas becomes overworked and exhausted.

Insidious sugar

Sugar is the greatest disturber of the body's energy production processes. And sugar is insidious. It is not only found in obvious foods such as sweets, cakes and canned drinks, but is also hidden in many other items such as ready meals, prepared sauces, most cereals, bread and pizzas. Sugar is everywhere.

To see how much sugar is in a food or drink that you consume regularly, take a look at the label. The ingredients are listed in order of quantity. On a bar of chocolate, you may well discover that sugar is its most abundant ingredient, while cocoa is much further down the list, begging the question, is it a chocolate bar or a sugar bar? When you look at the label on a ready-made food item, sugar is almost always present. It is worth asking *why* sugar is included in some dishes – if you were to cook the same food at home you would not add any sugar, so why do manufacturers? The reason is quite simple: they put sugar in food because it is relatively cheap and provides a familiar and allegedly enhanced flavour – but, as nutritionists, we maintain its inclusion is unnecessary.

Sugar in the morning, sugar in the evening

Often we have no idea how much sugar we are eating, because it is so often present in foods we do not expect to contain it. Look at a typical day: the Western daily breakfast of cereal, toast and coffee will probably contain sugar in at least two, if not three, of the items – sugar is present in bread and breakfast cereals, and may be added to coffee. This also holds true for a typical mid-morning snack of a couple of biscuits and a canned drink. Lunch of a sandwich, a cereal bar and another canned drink will have sugar in the bread, possibly in the sandwich filling, in the cereal (granola) bar and the canned drink. Chomping through a mid-afternoon snack of

Alcohol, in all forms, behaves like simple sugars as it is absorbed directly through the stomach and into the bloodstream. This is why drinking on an empty stomach can have such a rapid effect: the alcohol goes straight to the brain, affecting speech and judgement (especially when driving), and causing a loss of balance and coherence. If you are going to drink alcohol, make sure you eat something first, because this will slow down the release of alcohol into the bloodstream. However, drinking and driving,

To become more sugar-aware, try this experiment: avoid all sugar for two weeks. Eliminate sugar from tea and coffee, deny yourself chocolate bars and sweets, don't eat any honey and say 'no' to desserts. After two weeks have elapsed, try eating a spoonful of white sugar – the taste will seem overpoweringly sweet and it should turn you off sugar for quite a while.

biscuits, chocolate and tea piles on more sugar. Even the evening meal, perhaps pasta and a store-bought sauce, or maybe a ready-made meal, also has an extremely high sugar content.

You may also be surprised to find out how much sugar is lurking in foods we would consider to be healthy, such as yoghurt, some fruit juices, canned baked beans and other vegetables. Even the more natural forms of sugar, such as honey and molasses, will disturb blood-sugar balance. Eating such sugar-rich foods will raise your blood sugar levels, interfere with insulin release and stress your body.

regardless of what has been eaten, is obviously dangerous and illegal.

Most fruits are digested rapidly, particularly when eaten on an empty stomach, and can have a similar effect on blood-sugar balance to eating sugar, albeit to a lesser degree. Therefore people who suffer from fluctuations of energy, mood swings and fatigue would be ill-advised to follow diets where fruit is only eaten before midday. Although beneficial as antioxidants and a good source of fibre, fruit should be eaten in moderation when attempting to rebalance blood sugar levels – and in some cases, avoided.

What goes up, must come down

The most effective way of keeping your blood sugar levels constant is to avoid processed sugars and to include protein in every meal. Protein blood sugar levels. However, be aware that juicing raw vegetables, such as carrots, gives them a high glycaemic index, because the fibre content which slows digestion, and with it, sugar

---

Sugar release times

Foods release their sugars at different rates. The most beneficial are the moderate- to slow-release sugars, which provide a consistent release of sugar throughout the day. Avoid quick-release foods, which provide a sugar surge, but deplete the body's energy reserves very speedily, leaving you feeling even more tired than before.

Quick-release sugars
- honey
- canned drinks
- sweets and chocolate
- white rice and rice cakes
- french bread
- cornflakes
- baked potatoes
- raisins
- apricots
- dried fruits
- cooked root vegetables.

Moderate-release sugars
- popcorn
- corn chips
- brown rice
- pasta
- bagels

Slow-release sugars
- rye bread
- yoghurt (unsweetened)
- wholegrains such as millet, buckwheat, brown rice, quinoa
- legumes including kidney and lima beans, lentils and chick peas
- apples
- pears
- all raw root vegetables

---

encourages a series of hormonal secretions, which slow down the release of sugars. Protein sources such as nuts, legumes, beans, tofu, eggs, fish and poultry are ideal. For example, after a meal of a bowl of plain pasta with a tomato sauce, blood sugar will rise sharply, leading to a fall soon after. Adding some protein, such as tofu or chicken, will slow down the digestive process and help to create a more consistent blood sugar level. The protein should be combined with fibre, which slows down sugar release and makes successful blood-sugar management more likely.

Some foods are known to release their sugars quickly, while others do so more slowly. It is the latter that should make up the greater part of our diets. Foods all have what is known as a 'glycaemic value' and the higher the value, the more quickly the sugars in the food will affect

release, has been removed. The different rates of sugar release in various foods are outlined in the box above.

Sleeping tight – beating insomnia

Many of us experience the occasional sleepless night but, for some, this can be a regular occurrence, causing fatigue, irritability and affecting memory and concentration. Sleep is essential for body rebuilding. During the night, human growth hormone triggers proteins throughout the body to build new cells and repair any damage. It is only released when we sleep, so adequate daily (or nightly) rest is imperative to maintain a healthy body.

Stress and all stimulants, such as alcohol, tea, coffee and cola drinks, chocolate and drugs (both prescription and recreational), interfere with sound sleep patterns, as do heavy meals late

Energy-boosting snacks

The following healthy snacks are ideal for helping to rebalance blood sugar levels throughout the day.

- Almonds, chopped dates and an apple

- Dried fruit (limit consumption to once or twice a week)

- Natural low-fat yoghurt (sugar-free), with ground pumpkin seeds and wheatgerm

- Oat and wheatgerm flapjacks with dried fruit such as apricots

- Crispbread or oatcake with cheese

- Avocado dip with rice cakes or rye crispbread

- Raw vegetables with yoghurt or sour cream dip

- Cereal (granola) bars (sugar-free), with nuts and dried fruit

- Houmous and crispbread or oatcake

- Fruit topped with sesame seeds

Try this simple quiz to see how well you are managing your blood sugar

If blood sugar is raised rapidly, it will come crashing down with the release of insulin, leaving you tired and craving something to get you going again. This roller-coaster of blood-sugar highs and lows greatly affects our feelings and energy levels. Learning how to restore balance is one of the fundamental factors for good health.

1 Do you feel you need more than 7 hours' sleep a night?

2 Do you feel sluggish and heavy in the mornings?

3 Do you need a pick-me-up to start the day (tea, coffee, a cigarette)?

4 Do you drink tea and coffee regularly throughout the day?

5 Do you sip soft drinks (sodas) throughout the day?

6 Do you urinate frequently?

7 Do your palms sweat?

8 Do you smoke?

9 Do you look forward to an alcoholic drink in the evening?

10 Do you get very thirsty but find that the thirst is not relieved by drinking water?

11 Do you feel sleepy during the day?

12 Do you crave sugar, bread or carbohydrates through the day?

13 Do you avoid exercising, due to tiredness?

14 Do you lose concentration from time to time?

15 Do you get dizzy or irritable if you don't eat often?

If you have answered 'yes' to three or more of these questions, it is possible that you have a blood-sugar management problem. Try and follow our recommendations and see if there is an improvement.

If your score is above five, then blood sugar problems are more than likely. You should follow our recommendations. If there is no improvement, you should see your doctor and/or a nutritionist for further investigation.

in the evening, indigestion and poor blood-sugar management. Dietary factors are also implicated, so if you do not sleep well, it is worth examining what you eat later in the day.

Saturated fatty foods, such as dairy products, red meats and hard cheeses all take a considerable time for the body to digest, so it is advisable to avoid these in the evening. Instead it is preferable to choose grilled fish and vegetables, rice dishes and salads, as they are less taxing for the digestive system. After dinner, herbal teas such as peppermint (aids digestion) and camomile (relaxing) are perfect alternatives to caffeinated teas and coffees.

nutrition know-how

Eating fish with green vegetables for dinner will help promote a good night's sleep, as these foods are rich in calcium and magnesium, necessary both for brain chemistry balance and to relax the body.

Foods containing tyramine, an amino acid found in the nightshade family of vegetables, such as tomatoes, aubergines (eggplants), zucchini, potatoes and spinach, all stimulate the production of the hormone adrenaline, which may interfere with a good night's sleep. Tyramine is also found in alcohol, bacon, ham and sausage, so keeping these to a minimum at dinner is advisable.

The specific nutrients involved in sleep problems are the minerals calcium and magnesium. Any imbalance of these can precipitate mild to severe insomnia. It is worth avoiding foods that contain them to see if your sleep improves. Try omitting the following from your evening meal: broccoli, cauliflower, brussels sprouts, mackerel, peas, chicken, salmon, greens and kale.

Another amino acid, tryptophan, is produced by the brain to help regulate sleep. A rich supply of it is found in bananas, turkey, tuna, figs, dates, nut butters and wholegrain crackers. Including any of these foods with dinner, or as a late-night snack, will help to promote sound sleep.

PMS – The monthly monster

Not every woman suffers from premenstrual syndrome (PMS) but, for those who do, there often seems to be no escape from the monster that arrives with hideous, cyclical regularity. For some women, PMS is purely physical, causing a range of symptoms, particularly lower back pain, abdominal cramps, swollen and tender breasts and water retention. These range from being uncomfortable to extremely unpleasant.

For others, however, there are also emotional symptoms, which make PMS nothing short of a prison sentence. The symptoms can start anywhere from mid-cycle to just a few days before the onset of menstruation. For these women, irritability and mood swings, anger or violent outbursts – even thoughts of suicide – are features that the sufferer is unable to control, making her withdrawn and antisocial. These women often describe their experiences as 'having someone else move into my head', and they are frequently surprised by some of their own uncharacteristic behaviour. In many cases, it is husbands and partners who are the quickest to identify the symptoms and attribute them to their true cause.

Hormonal balance

One of the major causes of PMS is an imbalance of the hormones oestrogen and progesterone. Although such imbalances may be 'natural', in that they occur without outside triggers, there are also many other factors that can cause PMS.

Every day we are exposed to many products (such as plastic containers and food wraps) that have oestrogen-like properties that can upset the normal levels of oestrogen circulating in the body. Oestrogen naturally drops mid-cycle, to allow progesterone levels to increase (progesterone is the hormone that supports a potential pregnancy), so an excessive amount of oestrogen will disturb this delicate balance.

Poor blood-sugar management is also a contributing factor in PMS – eating a lot of sugar, simple carbohydrates and processed foods will adversely affect blood-sugar levels. Also, a high sugar intake depletes the body's stores of magnesium, a primary nutrient required for muscle relaxation. Therefore, period pains and cramps can be relieved by increasing magnesium-rich foods such as wholegrains, green leafy vegetables, dairy products, fish and seafood.

B-complex vitamins are necessary for relaxation, reduction of breast tenderness and water retention, support of the adrenal glands and stress management. Wholegrains are good sources: millet, rye, buckwheat and brown rice.

PMS and food cravings

Premenstrual food cravings are common – and they usually include stimulants such as tea, coffee and alcohol, all of which disturb blood-sugar management, stress hormone output, and consequently one's mood. Eating small meals regularly throughout the day will reduce cravings.

nutrition know-how

If you have difficulty sleeping through the night, don't battle with it – get up and prepare yourself a light snack of some dates and bananas, or a low-fat natural yoghurt with a teaspoon of nut butter. Better still, purée a little of all the above in a blender to make a 'midnight milkshake'.

Prior to menstruation, many women crave chocolate. The reason for this is that chocolate contains a significant amount of magnesium, as well as satisfying the immediate energy requirements that blood-sugar imbalances induce. But it is better to eat other magnesium-rich foods, such as apricots, figs or peaches, which will satisfy a sweet tooth without leaching away other vital nutrients. Combining any of these foods with a small protein snack such as almonds (which also contain magnesium) or other nuts or seeds, will help to balance blood sugar levels.

Is your child wild or mild?

There are several possible causes of hyperactivity in children. Some are linked to genetics or the environment, but by far the most prevalent cause, it appears, is the relationship that the nervous system has with certain foods.

Classic symptoms of hyperactivity include an inability to concentrate on any game or task for more than a few minutes at a time; having excessive spurts of energy followed by exhaustion; head-banging, aggressive behaviour towards other children (and adults); and being

Foods for memory and concentration

Whether you're studying hard for exams, spending 10 hours a day in the office, making a presentation, driving a car, or carrying out any activity that requires concentrated brain effort, the food you eat throughout the day will have a direct effect on your ability to concentrate and remember things.

Brain cells require **choline**, a B vitamin, for optimal function. Once present in the brain, it is transformed into acetyl choline, a neurotransmitter responsible for sending information from one brain cell to the next. Low levels of acetyl choline cause loss of memory in varying degrees – from the 'It's on the tip of my tongue…', to complete forgetfulness. Choline is also required for the formation and maintenance of the myelin sheath that protects the nerve cells, ensuring rapid and accurate transmission of information.

Choline-rich foods include calf's liver, cabbage, cauliflower, caviar, eggs, lentils and soya products, including tofu.

Another neurotransmitter, **dopamine**, requires vitamin B3 and iron for its formation. Dopamine is involved in the laying down and maintenance of memory.

Good food sources of B3 are brewer's yeast, turkey, halibut, pumpkin seeds and peanuts. Iron-rich foods include calf's liver, apricots (particularly when dried), raisins, pumpkin seeds and walnuts.

The B-complex vitamins (B1, B2, B3, B5, B6, B12, biotin and B9, folic acid) are all required for memory maintenance. Signs of deficiency in these vitamins include memory loss, poor concentration, impaired learning and general forgetfulness. B-complex vitamins are essential for the production of cellular energy – and nowhere more than in the brain cells.

Good food sources include brewer's yeast, chicken, collards, kale, oatmeal, soya beans, fish, avocado and potatoes.

easily frustrated and irritated. The child may also be unusually clumsy, restless at mealtimes, and underachieve at school. Repeated attempts at encouraging him/her to concentrate and focus, even for a few minutes at a time, usually prove to be infuriatingly futile.

Food management can help tremendously in controlling hyperactivity. Children respond very quickly to changes in diet and environment, and those foods that are affecting your child will hurriedly make themselves known if you follow a plan of first eliminating the food from the kitchen for a few weeks, and then re-introducing it. Working with hyperactive children like this is possibly one of the most effective ways of using food as therapy.

The first step is to keep a food diary to determine which foods seem to be having the greatest effect. To monitor changes in behaviour, it is essential to eliminate all sweetened foods, artificial, fruit-flavoured drinks, fizzy drinks and squashes, and all processed and packaged foods. Foods containing colourings, additives and a high level of sugars can all interfere with brain chemistry; this seems to affect some more dramatically than others.

In addition, salicylates (compounds found naturally in some foods, which act like aspirin), have been found to be a major culprit in upsetting the delicate brain chemistry of children. Salicylates are abundant in apricots, almonds, apples, cherries, currants, raisins, all berry fruits, peaches, plums, prunes, tomatoes and oranges. Often, simply removing citrus fruits and orange juice from the diet can have a profound effect on the child's behaviour. Essential fatty acids also play a large part in the management of hyperactivity. Required for nerve transmission, any imbalance or deficiency in essential fatty acids can affect the sensitive communication from one nerve ending to another. A high-sugar diet can interfere with the utilization of essential fats, causing incorrect or incomplete nerve transmission. Hyperactive children are frequently found to have a deficiency of the omega-3 group of essential fatty acids, and increasing foods that contain them is recommended. Oily fish such as tuna, sardines, salmon and mackerel are all rich in omega-3 fats, as are pumpkin and sunflower oils (which can be used in dressings, but should not be heated).

Green vegetables containing magnesium are often found to be lacking in a hyperactive child's diet, upsetting the fragile calcium/magnesium balance required for optimal brain and nerve function. Serving broccoli, peas, cauliflower, spinach and figs will help to increase intake of magnesium, as will wholegrains, including oats and brown rice.

There can be other causes for hyperactivity in a child. If adjusting your child's diet as discussed above does not make a significant difference to their behaviour, then environmental and toxic elements can be considered. It is advisable to consult a specialist in this field, and there are tests that can be carried out to determine if toxicity is the cause. Other influences include physical trauma, such as a fall, which may have caused unseen damage. Always consult a medical professional for advice.

managing stress

Stress is a modern buzzword, but do you really know what it means? To function as efficiently as possible, the body constantly strives to achieve a perfect balance in all its processes. Stress is any disturbance to that balance. The body has to work hard to combat the physical and emotional stress that it is bombarded with.

Stress is inevitable and can take many forms. It is difficult to imagine a life without it; each of us will find various things stressful at different times. There are two types of stress – external and internal. External (exogenous) stresses, which we are more familiar with, are imposed on the body from outside. Internal (endogenous) stresses occur inside the body. Both are outlined in the box on the right.

An ancient response to modern stress

To understand how stress can adversely affect the body, we need to look back in time. Early man's ability to survive depended on his skill at hunting and escaping predators. When confronted with the threat of attack, the body instantly reacts by releasing stress hormones that trigger the release of energy to the organs most involved in defending the body. This is called the 'fight or flight' response. Although not frequently confronted by wild animals today, we still react in this way to any perceived threat or challenge. When the hormones are released, the brain becomes more alert and the five senses function with a heightened level of skill.

Identify your stressors

External stresses	Internal stresses
● Pollution	● Food allergies and intolerances
● Hydrogenated fats	
	● Auto-immune disease
● Smoking and alcohol	
	● Metabolic waste
● Excessive exposure to the sun	
	● High cholesterol
● Heavy workload	● Blood sugar imbalances (and diabetes)
● Emotional problems	
	● Hormonal imbalances
● Bereavement	
	● Nutrient deficiencies
● Divorce/separation	
	● Depression caused by chemical imbalance

At the same time, stored glucose is released from the liver to fuel the skeletal muscles for exertion.

LEFT Potatoes are a rich source of vitamin C, which supports the adrenal system.

There are seven major changes that occur in the body when it reacts to stress, all stemming from the 'flight or fight' ability to react to danger. These are:

1 The heart rate goes up to pump extra blood, in order to supply vital nutrients required for energy production.

2 The breathing rate increases to allow more oxygen into the blood and more carbon dioxide to be excreted.

3 The blood vessels supplying the brain and muscles dilate to allow increased quantities of oxygen, glucose and nutrients to these vital areas.

As we can see, the 'fight or flight' reaction primes the body for action and is designed to do so for a short, concentrated period of time. But if the body is kept in this heightened state of alarm for long periods, it can damage its physical and emotional well-being. It is like putting your car in neutral and pressing one foot right down on the accelerator and the other on the brakes!

When this occurs, the body seeks to restore its natural balance and harmony, so it adjusts its parameters and adapts to the stress. For example, it may reset blood pressure, allowing it

The long-term effects of stress means we're constantly living on our nerves – and using up precious energy reserves.

4 The spleen produces more blood, carrying with it extra immune cells. The blood itself has a greater ability to clot in case of injury.

5 The liver and skeletal muscles release extra glucose into the blood to provide more energy.

6 The pupils dilate to allow more light into the eye to improve vision.

7 Digestion slows and digestive enzyme secretion is halted, freeing energy for use by the muscles and the brain.

to remain higher than usual, or it may readjust the glucose levels in the blood so that they are continuously being drained. Both, of course, are potentially dangerous.

But, back to the ancestors. After a period of stress, our ancestors rested to allow the body to restore its balance. All the symptoms in the 'fight or flight' response abated, reinstating the normal levels of hormones, blood glucose and digestion. Modern-day life doesn't allow us this luxury of recovery time. Our stresses are so abundant – and frequently continuous – that our bodies end up in a permanent state of 'fight or flight' reaction, without any respite. The long-term result of this is that we remain in high gear, using up our precious stores of glucose and energy. Our bodies never have the chance to rebalance themselves and physiological change can eventually occur. Some of the most common physiological effects of stress are listed below. Added to this, some of the foods we choose to eat also increase the stress on our overtaxed and drained bodies by depleting energy levels and providing insufficient nutrients.

experienced as the body moved into high gear. This is stress in action. However, by the second or third public speaking engagement, initial nerves will have receded and he or she is more likely to approach the task with a sense of calm. Therefore the stress experienced would be much less severe. The situation is the same, it is just the interpretation of it that has altered. If we acknowledge stress and understand that it can be altered, then we can find a way of minimizing it.

Food as a stressor

Foods that are not particularly good for us or to which we are allergic, can cause stress. In

Stress symptoms – the physiological effects of stress include:

- Immune suppression leading to frequent colds and flu
- Food cravings
- Weight loss
- Constant fatigue
- Loss of appetite
- Mood swings
- Depression
- Anxiety
- Skin irritation

Interpreting emotional stress

It is an interesting fact that emotional stress is experienced in a uniquely different way by everyone. What may be stressful to you may not be a problem for someone else. The stress of a certain situation may be lessened if we choose to view it differently. Let's use the example of speaking in public, which frightens many people. The very first time someone does this he or she will probably experience stress: the palms may sweat and an adrenaline rush would be

addition, faulty digestion, induced by poor dietary habits, bacterial or parasitic infections, will increase the likelihood of a leaky gut (see page 71, allowing unwanted food particles to pass into the bloodstream. This causes an immune response, which when it occurs daily, overworks the adrenal glands. Ironically, it is a catch-22 situation, as the adrenals respond to stress by releasing increased amounts of another hormone, cortisol, which aims to redress the balance. One of the side-effects of excess or repeated cortisol release is digestive disturbance. The cycle is self-perpetuating – and increasingly damaging to health.

Having a positive outlook on life can also help reduce stress. So what if you are stuck in traffic? It is not your fault so why not listen to some music or talk to your travelling companions. Do what you can to deal with it – use your cell phone if you have one to tell people why you are late, for example. If you can't do anything, try to accept it.

Stress, food and nutrition

So what can we do about all this? While we may not be able to influence many of the external factors that induce stress, we can at least help our body to cope with its effects.

Certain nutrients have been shown to help deal with stress and, at the same time, support the organs that are involved in the stress reaction. For example, the Fighting Five – vitamins A, C and E, and the minerals zinc and selenium – can disarm the free radicals that are produced if the body is under stress. Foods containing these vital antioxidants include plums, tomatoes, kiwi fruit, dark green vegetables, seafood, sesame seeds and pumpkin seeds.

Stress and the immune system

It is a well-known and well-documented fact that people affected by stress are more prone to illness. This is due to the dampening effect that long-term stress has on the immune system.

In times of increased stress, we get more colds, infections and, in more serious cases, the body does not deal with pre-cancerous cells with the same efficiency as in times of rest and relaxation. The heightened alertness of the body reduces the immune system's ability to fight infection, as the body deems this to be less important than dealing with the immediate danger it has sensed. The output of the immune system's battling killer cells and T-cells is suppressed, allowing invaders to flourish. As you can see, in periods of stress it is vital to support the immune system.

Immune system hormones

Two important hormones play a dramatic role in the immune system during periods of stress. These are dehydroepiandosterone (DHEA) and cortisol. Researchers have found that many people suffering chronic conditions have decreased levels of DHEA and increased levels of cortisol (these hormones can easily be measured using a simple saliva test). There are many reasons for the decline in DHEA. Stress acts on the adrenal glands to switch the production of DHEA to that of cortisol. This imbalance can have many consequences for the body, as well as suppressed immunity. DHEA levels decline as we age, and it is thought that we manufacture only 20 per cent as much in our seventies and eighties as we do in our teens and twenties. Declining levels have been linked to increased fat stores (especially around the abdomen), constant hunger, insomnia, lack of interest in sex and an increased incidence of allergies and infections.

If any of the symptoms apply to you, ask your nutritional consultant or health practitioner to test your levels of DHEA and cortisol. If these turn out to be low, as soon as adequate levels of DHEA are restored, the benefits will include improved cholesterol levels, increased bone

When this happens, both hormones may need temporary supplementation, carefully combined with specific herbal nutrients such as licorice and Siberian ginseng. This type of programme would need to be designed and supervised by a professional nutrition consultant.

In the US, it is possible to buy supplements of DHEA from pharmacies and some healthfood stores. However, in some countries only a doctor can prescribe DHEA or its precursor, pregnelolone, which acts in the same way.

Some foods stress the body. A deficiency of any nutrient is a stress in itself, because it places a strain on all the enzyme processes that depend upon it.

health and a better muscle-to-fat ratio. Cortisol can be a dangerous hormone. Increased levels of it are responsible for compromised thyroid function, impaired joint function and decreased energy. Furthermore, a higher amount of cortisol causes the breakdown of muscle and bone, eventually leading to the bone-thinning disease osteoporosis.

Boosting DHEA and reducing cortisol

The balance of DHEA and cortisol can be restored by supporting the adrenal glands with the foods recommended in the box on Stress-busters (see pages 60–61) and through relaxation techniques such as meditation or yoga.

In the most severe cases of damage caused by long-term stress, the adrenal glands reduce their production of both DHEA and cortisol. This stage is known as adrenal exhaustion or failure.

Managing stress through diet

So how do we set about managing stress? While it may not be possible to eliminate many of the external stresses that occur in our lives, we do have the power to alter our eating habits and make changes to our lifestyle.

Some foods we eat actually stress the body. A deficiency of any nutrient is a stress in itself, because it places a strain on all the enzyme processes that depend upon it. To support the important adrenal glands, the body needs the following vital vitamins and minerals: vitamin B5, vitamin C and magnesium. To help control the effects of the stress you are subjected to every day, it is essential to include plenty of foods containing these nutrients in your daily diet. The adrenal glands need abundant supplies of vitamin C, but this is the only vitamin that we cannot store in our bodies – we must obtain a regular daily supply from our diet. The richest sources include all black and red berries, kiwi fruit and citrus fruits, as well as potatoes and peppers – all produce that is easily available from supermarkets.

During periods of extreme stress, the requirement for this essential vitamin increases many times over. One of the most common symptoms of vitamin C deficiency is mouth problems such as ulcers (canker sores) and sores. These can be alleviated within 24 hours if optimal levels of the vitamin are supplied.

levels of sugars and refined carbohydrates depletes many stored nutrients, especially magnesium, and also puts excessive demands on the pancreas to produce large amounts of insulin (see Blood-sugar management, page 44). Over a period of time, the pancreas becomes fatigued and works less efficiently, in some cases leading to the early stages of maturity-onset diabetes.

Cutting out or reducing the amount of sugar that we eat can also have a profoundly beneficial effect on the liver, helping it to perform its detoxification processes more efficiently. The

Stress-busters

With a demanding work schedule, stopping for a relaxed and nutritious meal is one luxury few people can manage during the day. So in the morning, prepare some nutritious mini-meals to take to work. The following snacks are quick and easy to make and can be eaten 'on the run'.

Smoked mackerel pâté on wholegrain crackers

Almond butter on rye toast

Spinach salad with sunflower seeds

Magnesium is the primary mineral required by the adrenal glands and so magnesium-rich foods should be eaten daily. These include grains, green leafy vegetables, soya beans, wheatgerm, almonds, cod and mackerel. Good sources of vitamin B5 include wholegrains, green leafy vegetables, and animal and dairy products.

So, if certain foods are good for stress, it follows that there are also foods that have a negative effect and actually increase stress. Eating high

liver is the primary cleansing organ in the body. Its job is to continuously filter the blood to remove all potentially harmful toxins, waste matter and debris produced by natural processes. Reducing any of the stresses put upon the liver therefore, will be a tremendous help to its ability to function. Also, stimulant drinks such as tea, coffee and alcohol rob the body of nutrients and encourage the production of adrenaline, so cutting your intake of these is a positive step to controlling your stress.

Needless to say, it is also a good idea to limit, or eliminate, your intake of refined, processed and convenience foods, as they have a lot of artificial preservatives, salt and sugar in them and their nutritional content is usually very, very low.

Weekend destressing plan

For increased energy, and as a way to detoxify a stressed system, set aside a long weekend when you can allow yourself to do very little. Fill your kitchen with plenty of fresh fruits and vegetables, and limitless mineral water. During the weekend, aim to eat and drink only foods in

This is particularly beneficial after a bout of excessive eating and/or drinking.

Virtually all vegetables can be juiced, as well as fruits. You should aim to drink between three and four green vegetable juices per day. The best juicing vegetables include watercress, parsley, spinach, zucchini, green peppers and lettuce. As fruits are high in fructose, it is advisable to dilute fruit juices 50 per cent with water.

Spend plenty of time resting, go for some gentle walks, and be sure to get lots of sleep. By the

Soya milkshake with fresh berries

Potato salad with rollmop herrings

Strawberry and kiwi fruit salad with soya cream

Mango smoothie with soya milk and sunflower seeds

a raw state: these will provide an abundance of nutrients that will help to combat stress.

Start each morning with 3 cups of boiled water, and drink it as hot as you can comfortably stand. You may add either a slice of lemon, or 2–3 slices of fresh raw ginger to the water to add flavour, but this should be drunk before anything else. This tonic has a cleansing effect on the liver, and induces the production of bile, to clear any backlog in the common bile duct.

second day it is possible that you will experience a headache or some muscle aches and pains, but this is not a bad sign – it shows that your body is detoxifying itself. Remember that you will reap the benefits at the beginning of the following week, when you will feel as if you have been away on vacation! Throughout, ensure that you drink plenty of water. You could also arrange a shiatsu or aromatherapy massage for the second or third days – an enjoyable way to assist the detoxification process.

managing depression

Depression is not unusual. In fact, it has become so prevalent in the Western world that the names of antidepressant drugs, such as Prozac, are now familiar to most people. Depression and anxiety have many possible causes, but it may surprise you to learn that they can be brought on by a reaction to food.

We all feel depressed from time to time, but we can usually link our unhappiness to an event or set of circumstances. However, many people suffer from depression that has no identifiable cause. This can range from feeling a bit down to being unhappy all the time and, in extreme cases, to not being able to experience any joy in life or to find any reason for living. Feeling down is usually transitory and will improve when life circumstances or mental attitudes change. However, the last three instances are more serious and require attention and treatment.

Food influences our brain chemistry. Some foods promote a feeling of well-being while others can 'bring us down' and suppress positive emotions. Ironically, many of the foods that make us feel good are not especially beneficial to our health, and therefore, as with many areas of nutrition, the aim is to find a healthy balance.

Carbohydrates and mood

When we eat foods containing carbohydrates and sugar, they encourage the absorption of tryptophan into the brain. Tryptophan is a mood-lifting amino acid that is contained in protein foods. Eating carbohydrates allows tryptophan to be more readily absorbed. Bananas, turkey, cottage cheese and dried dates contain high levels of tryptophan.

All nerve impulses in the brain are carried between the nerve cells by substances known as neurotransmitters. Tryptophan is a precursor to

Depression checklist

Use this checklist to find out if you likely to be suffering from depression

Are you:
- finding it difficult to get out of bed in the mornings?
- having problems concentrating?
- suffering from a recent major loss or breakdown of a relationship?
- lacking the energy to participate in things that usually interest you?
- losing your appetite?
- craving sweet foods?
- tearful for no apparent reason?
- living in a country where sunlight is limited?
- feeling hopeless, or that there is no point in life?

If you have answered 'yes' to three of more questions, you may be depressed.

Consult your medical doctor and if depression is diagnosed, work with him or her in addition to your nutrition consultant.

the neurotransmitter called serotonin – low levels of which have long been associated with depression and anxiety. Antidepressants such as Prozac affect serotonin levels in the brain. This type of antidepressant belongs to a group of drugs known as Selective Serotonin Re-uptake Inhibitors (SSRIs). These work by inhibiting the re-uptake of serotonin in the brain, allowing it to remain available and so to produce a feeling of well-being.

Vitamin B6 is also involved with the synthesis of serotonin. Ensuring that your diet is rich in foods containing B6 (see chart, right) could help to lift mild depression.

It is no coincidence that when we are feeling depressed, the foods we crave are likely to be sweet ones – ice-cream, chocolate or cakes. These foods directly affect brain chemicals. Think what happens when dieting: these carbohydrate-rich foods are removed, inevitably leading to a craving for them – as mood dips and the food cravings become stronger, this ultimately leads to the failure of the diet.

Dopamine and depression

Low levels of dopamine are linked with the incidence of depression, while increased levels can bring about feelings of well-being. Although not strictly a neurotransmitter, dopamine acts like one in that it helps nerve impulses in the brain to cross the tiny gap that separates them.

Dopamine is synthesized from tyrosine, an amino acid found in protein foods. It requires the vitamins B12 and B9 (more commonly known as folic acid), as well as the mineral magnesium, for its production.

Foods rich in tyrosine include almonds, avocados, bananas, cottage cheese, lima beans, peanuts (raw and unsalted), pumpkin seeds and sesame seeds. Foods high in vitamin B12 include fish, dairy products and spirulina (although it is not clear whether humans can absorb B12 from spirulina). Those high in folic acid include calf's

B-vitamin boosters

Vitamin B1 (thiamine)

Found in brewer's yeast, brown rice, wheatgerm and soya beans.

Vitamin B3 (niacin or niacinamide)

Found in fish, eggs, brewer's yeast, wholegrains and poultry.

Vitamin B6

Found in wholegrains such as millet, buckwheat and oats, as well as shellfish such as prawns (shrimp), lobster and mussels.

Vitamin B12 (cyanocobalamine)

Found in fish and dairy products.

The zinc link

The link between zinc levels and depression is a strong one. Very often we see clients with anxiety or depression who show signs of zinc deficiency. Post-partum depression (commonly known as the 'baby blues') has also been attributed to zinc levels, as zinc reserves pass from the mother to the foetus a day or so before birth. Zinc is the basis for the baby's growth and immune system. Replacing the mother's lost zinc after the birth can help conquer depression.

You can carry out a simple test to check if your zinc levels are adequate by answering the questions opposite. If you do decide to increase zinc, no more than 50mg a day should be obtained from all sources (including those provided in a multivitamin supplement). We suggest that you consult a professional nutrition consultant before undertaking any supplementation.

Foods full of zinc include oysters, endive, alfalfa sprouts, seaweed, brown rice, asparagus, mushrooms, turkey and radishes.

Test your zinc levels

Check your own zinc levels by answering the following questions.

Do you...

- have white marks on your fingernails?
- rarely feel hungry?
- have pale skin?
- have stretchmarks around the abdomen or back?
- have oily skin, perhaps with some acne?
- suffer from frequent colds or flu?

If you answer 'yes' to two or more of these questions, you may well have a deficiency of zinc, in which case we recommend you include some zinc-rich foods in your daily diet. Zinc levels can be more accurately tested by analyzing the mineral content of a tiny cutting of hair from the nape of the neck. Most nutrition consultants will be able to arrange this test for you. It is easy to perform and relatively inexpensive.

liver, soya flour, green leafy vegetables (especially broccoli), eggs and brown rice. A good supply of magnesium can be obtained from sunflower seeds, green leafy vegetables, wheatgerm, soya beans, mackerel, swordfish and cod.

Depression and nutrient deficiency

There is a correlation between levels of some vitamins (especially B-complex) and depression.

Blood plasma levels of these nutrients have been shown to be low in those suffering from depression, and many people have reported that their symptoms improve when they increase their intake of foods with plentiful B vitamins. Vitamin B3 has been shown to be the most effective in managing depression, along with B6 and zinc. Try eating some vitamin B-rich foods every day to see if it helps lift your mood.

Depression and food allergies

Many clients come to see us for advice on coping with depression. Often, simple food allergies or intolerances are the culprits and, once identified, the problem can be remedied easily. Symptoms range from dark circles under the eyes to skin problems, insomnia, irritability, and anxiety.

The trigger foods can be highlighted by a simple blood test. However, in many cases it is easier to remove one or all of the most likely allergens from the diet. In our experience, this process of removal and replacement has shown some remarkable results.

The most common allergens in Europe are wheat, dairy products and citrus fruits, while in the US corn replaces wheat as the most prevalent allergen (see Inflammation, pages 91–97). Many other foods can be responsible, including 'fast' foods or 'junk' foods, colourings and additives. However, we have known of incidences of more unlikely foods being responsible for patients' misery, such as celery or tomatoes.

One example of a food allergy that has a strong link with depression is gluten allergy, which causes coeliac disease (see page 74). If people with this severe sensitivity to all gluten grains do not avoid gluten in their diets, they are more likely to suffer from depression.

While we have seen depressed clients get excellent results by avoiding certain foods, it is still advisable to seek the advice of your doctor if you are depressed, especially if you have been so for a long time.

nutrition know-how

Our grandmothers knew that an apple a day was a good thing: this holds true today. Apples contain pectin, which helps to remove lead from the digestive tract – important to those who live in traffic-saturated urban areas.

Tips for fighting depression

● Poor circulation can decrease the level of oxygen and nutrients required by the brain – so get up and get moving. Circulatory problems are discussed in more depth on page 114.

● You can improve your circulation by eating foods rich in the Fighting Five antioxidants (vitamins A, C, E and the minerals selenium and zinc) found in fresh fruits and vegetables, fish and grains. Iron is also required, as it is essential for the formation of the red blood cells that carry the nutrients in the blood. Offal (organ meats, such as liver), is a rich source of iron, as are apricots and raisins.

● Blood sugar is often a factor in depression (see Blood-sugar management, page 44). By learning to choose foods that release their sugars evenly throughout the day, you can avoid the highs and lows of the blood-sugar roller-coaster. Eat foods containing complex carbohydrates, found in all grains and vegetables, combined with a small amount of protein from animal foods, dairy produce, nuts or seeds. These will help keep your blood-sugar levels balanced all day long.

part two

Ailments and Remedies

the digestive system

Digestion is a complicated process that the body carries out continually – during every minute of the day, whether we're sleeping, working, exercising, or resting. Stress, however, interferes with the digestive processes, slowing it down or even halting it altogether.

During the 'fight or flight' response, the digestive system shuts down to allow energy to be diverted to where it is more immediately required – for movement, attack or defence. Understanding this shows us how the whole digestive system is put under pressure when we eat 'on the run'.

The type of meals that we eat can also either help or hinder the digestive process. Foods such as fruits, vegetables, wholegrains, nuts, seeds and A-grade protein (see page 45) promote efficient digestion. A diet high in saturated fats, meat, sugar, caffeine and convenience foods slows digestion, affecting general health and reducing the absorption levels of essential nutrients.

The digestive process

In order to understand digestive disorders, we need to know how the digestive system works. The process of digestion starts with the very first thought or smell of food. The brain sends messages to the salivary glands in the mouth to release additional digestive enzymes. This is why you salivate more at the thought of food.

These digestive enzymes are both abundant and powerful, quickly reducing most carbohydrates – such as fruit, vegetables, grains and cereals – to a pulp when combined with the chewing process. Meat, nuts and other proteins are more difficult to break down, requiring stronger, more acidic enzymes, such as those found in the stomach. Thorough chewing is important for crushing solid food particles, increasing the production of salivary enzymes and keeping the teeth clean and sharp. Most people do not chew their food adequately, placing more strain on the digestive system and increasing the likelihood of heartburn and indigestion.

The stomach is pivotal to the whole of the digestive process. It sits behind the ribcage, to the centre of the breastbone. No two people's stomachs are the same: posture, size and height all influence its shape. Sitting upright while eating ensures that the stomach has adequate space to perform its functions. The stomach releases hydrochloric acid, and is the most acidic environment in the body. (Abundant mucus is also produced, to protect the stomach lining

LEFT Ginger helps to quell indigestion and motion sickness.

from being damaged by its own acid.) The acid gets to work on proteins, while the complex arrangement of stomach muscles contract and relax to churn the food around until it is broken down into chyme.

Several factors can adversely affect the production of hydrochloric acid, such as increasing age, recreational and prescription drugs, smoking, alcohol and stress. This lack of acid can have long-lasting negative effects on digestion and absorption, causing many obvious (and some seemingly unrelated) health problems – see box below.

Hydrochloric acid in the stomach also kills off any ingested bacteria and parasites. It is the first line of defence of the intricate immune system that lines the entire length of the digestive tract. From the age of about 30 onwards, the acid levels tend to diminish, explaining the increasing amount of digestive imbalances and food intolerances that occur as we get older.

A very aggressive bacteria, *Helicobactor pylori,* can survive in this environment. If untreated, it can cause damage, and therefore requires rigorous antibiotic treatment.

The stomach also produces digestive enzymes. Pepsin further breaks down protein foods, making them easier for the intestines to digest. (Vitamin B6 is required to help this process: consuming plenty of sunflower seeds, kidney beans, barley, broccoli and cauliflower will boost existing levels.) Lipase starts off the process of digesting fats.

The final process that occurs in the stomach is the binding of vitamin B12, an extrinsic factor, to the intrinsic factor produced in the stomach, allowing it to be absorbed by the intestines. Vitamin B12 is vital for energy production, growth, and the formation of blood and cells.

As we age, levels of intrinsic factor fall, affecting the absorption of vitamin B12 and increasing the possibility of pernicious anaemia (vitamin B12 deficiency). This is why doctors sometimes give B12 injections to people who have been ill, the elderly, or those who are recuperating from surgery. Hydrochloric acid and digestive enzymes will also boost the stomach's own production of vitamin B12, as well as ensuring better protein digestion. To increase your vitamin B12 levels, eat more cottage cheese, haddock, halibut, chicken and tuna.

Symptoms of faulty digestion

- Burping
- Food allergies
- Indigestion
- Rectal itching
- Iron deficiency
- Nausea

- Bloating
- Headaches
- Vitamin B12 deficiency
- Cracked fingernails
- Intestinal parasites

- Stomach upsets
- Constipation
- Gas after meals
- Acne
- Chronic candida

The small intestine

This is the main area for digestion and absorption. Digestive enzymes that work on fats, proteins and carbohydrates are secreted from the pancreas and further break down the partially digested food matter (chyme) released from the stomach, preparing it for absorption in the three different sections of the small intestine: the duodenum, the jejunum and the ileum. Together, the total length of these sections is about 7m (23ft), but they are all tightly coiled around themselves within the abdominal cavity.

Within the internal face of the three sections, the surface area for digestion and absorption is increased by minute, finger-like projections called villi. They secrete enzymes, absorb essential nutrients and prevent food particles and other potentially threatening substances from getting into the bloodstream. This sensitive procedure can be upset by antibiotics and other drugs, alcohol, and/or a high intake of sugar. When reacting to such substances, the minute gaps between the cells of the villi become inflamed and widen, allowing unwanted food particles to pass into the bloodstream. This is called intestinal permeability, or a 'leaky gut', and can lead to food intolerances resulting in other immune responses such as headaches, fatigue, skin problems and arthritic types of pain in bone and muscle anywhere in the body.

The duodenum is the entry point for bile, produced in the liver and then concentrated and stored in the gall bladder. Bile is essential for breaking down particles of partially digested fats, allowing them to be absorbed. The pancreas releases bicarbonates to neutralize or reduce the acidity of stomach secretions, and also produces three digestive enzymes – protease to digest protein, lipase for fats and amylase for carbohydrates.

nutrition know-how

To help heal stomach ulcers, drink potato water every day (boil potato peelings and strain off the liquid) or potato juice (juice raw potatoes and add carrot or celery for flavour). Never use potatoes with green skin.

The jejunum and ileum are the major sites for the absorption of the remaining nutrients, including proteins, amino acids, water-soluble vitamins, cholesterol and bile salts.

The ileo-caecal valve

To separate the small and large intestines and to prevent any faecal matter from passing back up into the small intestine, a tight, one-way valve lies between them. This is the ileo-caecal valve, which is located very close to the appendix. It is an area that can easily become inflamed, as bacteria and parasites often adhere to its walls.

If inflammation occurs over a prolonged period, the ileo-caecal valve may stay open, allowing toxic matter up into the highly absorptive area of the ileum. This can lead to mistaken diagnosis of appendicitis, resulting in the unnecessary removal of the appendix, an important organ of lymphatic tissue. Treatment to kill the parasites or bacteria, and the removal of any potentially irritating foods (such as grains, pulses [legumes] and large amounts of fibre) for a short period, can remedy this minor problem without the need for invasive procedures.

The large intestine

The large intestine, also known as the colon, is made up of three consecutive sections (the ascending, transverse and descending colon), ending in the bowel and anus. Its muscular structure contracts and relaxes every few seconds to move the remaining matter – water, bacteria, insoluble fibre and waste products derived from the digestion process – to be excreted from the anus. This waste material is known as faeces.

Right from the start, when a mouthful of food is swallowed, the whole digestive process relies on a series of muscle contractions and relaxations to move food through the system, rather like the way a snake moves across the ground.

It is important to recognize the urge to go to the toilet and respond to it, as holding back faecal matter for even a couple of hours causes a greater absorption of water, which results in drier and more constipated stools. This is one of main causes of haemorrhoids.

It is 'normal' to have at least one bowel movement a day or more. Those with an efficient digestive system may 'go' after every meal. It is not uncommon, however, for several days to pass without a bowel movement, allowing toxic waste matter to be reabsorbed through the intestinal wall back into the bloodstream. This is a frequent cause of fatigue, headaches, nausea and feeling under the weather, explaining why a doctor will always ask a patient about bowel movements, even for a seemingly unrelated ailment. The problems related to constipation are discussed further on.

A healthy large intestine

To keep the large intestine healthy and functioning well, you should eat vegetables, fruit and insoluble fibre (derived from grains and pulses [legumes]) every day. These foods all contain magnesium, which keeps the muscles of the large intestine functioning well. While drinking juices made from liquidized fruit and vegetables provides an excellent source of magnesium, you should still eat several helpings per day of each in their whole form, as it is their fibrous content that helps to remove toxic waste matter from the large intestine, as well as encouraging regular muscle contraction and relaxation.

People who undergo any form of abdominal surgery have to be very careful with what they eat after the operation, as the natural process of elimination can be seriously disturbed for several days. Patients should be given simple meals for the first couple of days which do not tax the large intestine, decreasing the likelihood of constipation. Vegetable soups, salads, lightly steamed vegetables and rice are the best foods at this time as they are nutritionally rich, easily digested and absorbed and contain the necessary fibre to stimulate the colon's return to normal.

Digestive immunity

Between 60-70 per cent of the body's immune system is in the digestive tract – but this is not surprising if you consider the multitude of potentially harmful substances and bacteria that enter the body through the first part of the digestive system: the mouth. There are billions of protective bacteria living in the mouth, oesophagus and small intestine, and literally trillions in the large intestine. As the stomach is such a highly acidic environment, fewer protective bacteria are required, as most invaders cannot survive there.

Some 400–500 different types of bacteria have been identified in the gut, some of which are anti- and some pro-cancerous; some that synthesize vitamins B, A and K; some that produce substances to fight specific infections; and others that digest lactose (milk sugars) and regulate muscle contraction and relaxation. They produce natural antibiotics and anti-fungals to prevent the growth of unwelcome bacteria and fungus, as well as breaking down the toxic waste produced by invading bacteria, which is potentially more harmful than the bacteria themselves. They do this by producing large amounts of acid.

The protective bacteria also play an important role in guarding against the potentially harmful effects of toxic metals that get into the body, such as mercury from amalgam fillings and contaminated fish, radiation (from anti-cancer treatment; also found in some foods), and the pesticide and herbicide residues in most non-organic produce. Some bacteria are also

responsible for manufacturing hydrogen peroxide, in the presence of which cancer cells cannot survive. However, there are many factors that can disrupt the balance of these essential bacteria, as outlined in the box below.

The protective gut bacteria will remain dominant in the digestive tract, provided that it is a friendly environment undisturbed by an accumulation of harmful factors (see below). If, however, you are eating a poor diet, consuming alcohol regularly, living under constant stress, using antacids and painkillers on a frequent basis, and taking frequent courses of antibiotics prescribed by your doctor, that delicate balance will be thrown out. The 'bad' bacteria then have a chance to override the beneficial bacteria.

This type of lifestyle is very common – in fact, for many people, it is normal. Those who identify with it will also suffer from frequent indigestion, bloating and gas – and wonder why. The answer is simple. Their intestinal bacteria are at war.

Over the next six pages, we will examine a number of common digestive diseases in a little more detail.

Lifestyle factors affecting digestive efficiency

- Antibiotics
- High-fat diet
- Sugar
- Processed foods
- Anti-inflammatories
- Fried foods
- Alcohol
- Canned drinks (sodas)
- Stress
- Bereavment
- Smoking
- Recreational drugs

conditions

Constipation

The main cause of constipation is dehydration. Also, constipation is one of the foremost reasons for frequent headaches. It is essential to drink between 1.5–2 litres (3–4 pints) of still mineral water every day to satisfy the body's minimum requirements and to prevent constipation. If exercising, this intake should be doubled. Other causes of constipation are a high-protein diet without sufficient vegetable fibre, high intake of alcohol, tea, coffee and caffeinated drinks, all of which are dehydrating.

To avoid constipation, it is essential that the diet contains lots of soluble fibre, derived from fruits and vegetables, plus insoluble fibre from rice, barley, buckwheat and other grains. (If you are constipated and not drinking enough liquids, pulses and legumes will only exacerbate the problem, causing solids to build up.)

Constipation is more common during pregnancy and is often caused by taking iron supplements. Eating dried apricots that have been soaked overnight tackles both of these problems, as apricots are one of the highest fruit sources of iron and are also mildly laxative. However, if you are pregnant, do not stop taking iron tablets in order to replace them with natural sources, unless you have the agreement of your doctor.

Candida

This is a much talked-about problem affecting a large number of people. It is not well understood, but is thought to be mainly due to diet and lowered immunity. *Candida albicans* is naturally present in the digestive tract and is not harmful unless the immune system is compromised or a high-sugar diet is consumed. If this happens, it mutates into a potentially damaging fungus. The first signs of candida overgrowth include bloating, excessive gas and abdominal cramps that occur after eating fruit and other sweet foods. If the condition continues unchecked, it can lead to serious fatigue and mild depression. Some of the less obvious symptoms of candida overgrowth include insomnia, itchy ears, aching shoulders, irritability, lack of concentration, sore throat, muscle pain, hyperactivity and acne.

One of the main causes of candida overgrowth is the frequent use of antibiotics. While they are essential for stamping out persistent infections, antibiotics also kill off all the bacteria in the gut, including protective bacteria. This allows *Candida albicans* to multiply – often described as a 'yeast overgrowth'. See the Lifestyle Questionnaire on page 8 for information on the relationship between yeast overgrowth and various health problems.

Coeliac disease

Coeliac disease is a disease of the intestines in which the villi (the tiny hair-like protrusions that absorb nutrients from food) are flattened after coming into contact with gluten. Coeliac disease can cause malnutrition, diarrhoea, weight loss or just a general failure to thrive. This condition is quite common and is thought to run in families. In babies, it will usually manifest itself within a few weeks of the infant being introduced to solids containing gluten, but it can be triggered off at any stage in life.

Sufferers are allergic to gluten in all forms, so they should avoid wheat, barley, oats and rye. The traditional treatment for coeliac disease requires the cutting out of all starches and grains, including rice, potatoes and corn, in addition to gluten. Some people still do this, although nowadays it is not thought to be necessary. Many sufferers maintain an excellent level of health, as their diets tend to include a large proportion of fresh fruit and vegetables, as well as fish, chicken and gluten-free grains.

Diverticulitis

In this condition, the sensitive membranes that line the large intestine become inflamed, leading to the formation of small pouches. These pouches can easily fill with waste, which can then become infected, causing pain and further inflammation. Unless dietary measures are taken, diverticulitis can result in the need for emergency surgery.

The symptoms of diverticulitis include diarrhoea or constipation, tenderness, bloating, and most commonly, a frequent feeling of needing to go to the toilet. Regularly becoming constipated increases the likelihood of diverticulitis, so it is important to ensure that the diet is rich in fibre, water and essential fats.

Nutritional treatment for diverticulitis includes increasing water and fibre intake, reducing carbohydrates (especially the simple ones) and eating more A-grade proteins (see page 45). Home-made soups of liquidized vegetables make an excellent food during an attack, as they contain abundant nutrients that can be easily absorbed without further irritating the gut.

Diarrhoea

There are many possible causes for diarrhoea and it is more likely to be a symptom of another problem rather than a condition in itself. However, acute diarrhoea is usually the result of an infection. Bloody diarrhoea is a sign of serious inflammation and must be investigated by a doctor.

Intermittent bouts of diarrhoea may be caused by food allergies, parasitic infections, excessive caffeine consumption, pancreatic problems or stress levels.

Diarrhoea robs the body of large amounts of water, and with it valuable minerals. Always make sure you replace these after an attack by eating mineral-rich foods such as nuts, green vegetables and perhaps seaweed. Lost potassium must be replaced at once: abundant sources are avocados, chard, lentils, parsnips, spinach, most fresh nuts, sardines and bananas.

If you occasionally get diarrhoea, the culprit may well be food, so change your diet and monitor whether or not there is an improvement. If there is not, consider consulting a nutrition consultant and/or your doctor.

Food poisoning

Food poisoning occurs when a toxic substance is consumed, most often some form of bacteria. Symptoms can be apparent within a few minutes of ingesting the offending food, although it can take up to one week for some strains of bacteria to manifest themselves. This makes it less likely that the sufferer will attribute the illness to the guilty food. So it is quite possible that food contamination is more widespread than is currently believed.

There are numerous strains of food-poisoning bacteria, ranging from *Salmonella typhimurium* and *Escherichia coli* (*E. coli*) to *Clostridium botulinim*. Symptoms of food poisoning include chills, fever, chronic diarrhoea and muscle paralysis. There may well be frequent nausea and vomiting as well.

If you suspect that you may have been affected by contaminated food, seek medical advice. Nutritional aids to recovery include garlic, a powerful detoxifier, and potassium-rich foods, such as fruits and green leafy vegetables, to help replace lost minerals. Live bio yoghurt should help to re-establish the beneficial bacteria that live in the gut. Charcoal tablets (from health-food stores) can minimize the effects of many toxins, so take them at the first sign of poisoning.

Reduce the likelihood of food poisoning by taking sensible precautions. If you have any concerns about a food, then do not eat it! However, taking a garlic tablet before eating can help to detoxify pathogens. While you have little control over what a restaurant serves you, at home you can take avoidance measures. Follow the food hygiene tips listed in the box below.

Heartburn and indigestion

Heartburn is characterized by pain that appears to rise from the stomach towards the throat, together with a feeling of acidity. Indigestion is similar, but the sensation is static.

The traditional treatment for heartburn and indigestion is to take an antacid, yet this does carry some risk, as continued use of antacids disturbs the delicate acid/alkaline balance (Ph) of the body. The buffering systems that the body employs to rebalance Ph become stressed,

---

Basic food hygiene

• **Wash your hands before handling food.**

• **Always keep food hot or cold, not at room temperature.**

• **Ensure that all cooked foods are evenly and thoroughly heated.**

• **If eating outdoors, ensure that the food is well chilled and then eaten immediately after it is set out. Do not allow the food to sit in the sun.**

• **Do not buy food in cans that are damaged or swollen, even if the store is offering them at a bargain price. No amount of discount is worth the risk of severe food poisoning.**

• **Do not let raw meat come into contact with other foods during storage or preparation. Keep two or three separate chopping boards specifically designated for different foods. Wash your hands after handling raw meat.**

and if combined with a high-calcium diet, the kidneys can be damaged.

We see many clients whose condition is attributable to diet. If you are prone to indigestion or heartburn, try simplifying your meals. If you are eating many proteins, raw and cooked foods at one sitting, it can overload the digestive system. Foods should be eaten slowly and properly chewed. Avoid swallowing anything scalding hot or freezing cold. If you have continued problems, visit your nutrition consultant, because a food intolerance or enzyme deficiency could be involved.

If you suddenly develop indigestion which is severe and persistent, you should check with your doctor to rule out serious causes.

Hiatus hernia

A hiatus hernia occurs when the stomach bulges up into the chest, allowing food from the stomach to go back up into the oesophagus. Symptoms include heartburn, indigestion, belching and a burning sensation due to stomach acid coming into contact with the delicate oesophagel membrane which, in the long term, can cause oesophaegal ulcers.

Drinking aloe vera juice twice a day will help soothe the area. This can be bought in most healthfood stores and the flavoured variety is usually the most palatable.

Zinc is essential for tissue repair, and good food sources are pumpkin seeds, wholegrains, eggs and turkey, as well as shellfish such as oysters, lobsters, mussels and crabs.

Haemorrhoids

With haemorrhoids, the veins around the anus become enlarged. This common condition can be the cause of much pain and discomfort. Symptoms include anal swelling, irritation, burning and some bleeding. (Always remember that blood in the stools should be investigated by a doctor.)

A diet low in fibre and water can be responsible for haemorrhoids, as straining to defecate causes unnecessary pressure on the veins. Boosting fibre by eating more green vegetables and whole grains will soften faeces and make them easier to pass. Calcium and magnesium-rich foods assist healing. Good sources include vegetables, nuts and seeds. Severe, debilitating haemorrhoids require medical treatment.

Irritable bowel syndrome

It is estimated that as many as 15 per cent of the population of the UK and 20 per cent of the US population suffer from irritable bowel syndrome (IBS). With IBS, the movement of the digestive tract is disturbed, upsetting its natural rhythm. The passage of food is therefore interrupted, and this leads to a build-up of toxins and waste. Symptoms of IBS include pain, bloating, diarrhoea and/or constipation. Malabsorption of nutrients is also common.

nutrition know-how

Blackcurrants have anti-laxative properties and are very good for fighting diarrhoea. The vitamin C content of canned berries is almost as high as that of fresh. Blackcurrant herbal tea is also beneficial.

It is important to restore natural muscle tone in the gut, and the B-complex vitamins are most useful for this. These can be found in the following: wholegrains, fish, eggs and wheatgerm. Eating live bio yoghurt daily can help to promote the growth of friendly gut bacteria – this is vital for the digestive system, and also the synthesis of B vitamins. It is believed that sufferers of IBS require higher amounts of protein: A-grade protein sources such as tofu, fish and chicken are best.

nutrition know-how

Apples stimulate the growth of beneficial bacteria in the large intestine. They also contain pectin, which helps remove excess cholesterol and toxic metals from the digestive tract.

Peptic/duodenal ulcer

In this painful condition, the lining of the stomach or duodenum is eroded, leading to irritation of the tissues. The key symptom is a burning pain, especially one that comes on after eating. Ulcers are associated with stress, because stress can adversely affect stomach acid levels. Remedies include taking antacids (but these have side-effects – see page 76), or drinking large quantities of water to dilute the acid and so reduce the pain.

Avoiding processed foods, salt, spices, coffee and fried foods should offer some relief from pain and work to prevent future attacks. It is better to have frequent small meals throughout the day, consisting of wholegrains, steamed vegetables and a little A-grade protein, rather than three large meals. Cabbage juice, drunk daily, is an effective remedy for ulcers because it contains the amino acid methionine, which supports detoxification by the liver. As with heartburn, someone developing severe acid pain, especially if they are over 30, and losing weight, should consult their doctor in order not to miss a serious cause.

Parasites

There are many unwanted parasites that can get into the digestive system. These include threadworms, pinworms and tapeworms. It should be noted that the presence of parasites in the gut is not uncommon. They can be involved in numerous health issues, from depression to bloating. If you believe that you have parasites, we suggest that you work closely with your doctor and a nutrition consultant.

Crohn's disease

Crohn's disease can affect both the small and large intestines, causing inflammation, thickening and ulceration. The symptoms include weight loss, frequent and severe diarrhoea, persistent stomach distention and apparent food intolerances manifesting as chronic fatigue, aching muscles, skin rashes and acne. In severe cases, surgical removal of parts of the small intestine may be required.

Nutritional management can be a highly effective. This usually requires the omission of wheat and dairy products to reduce inflammation and excess mucus. Other food intolerances are usually found to aggravate the disease, including citrus fruit, tomatoes, spicy food, black peppercorns, coffee, cola drinks and alcohol, and so these have to be screened out.

The most important area to address is the inflammation caused by Crohn's disease. During the first few months it is essential to reduce the intake of insoluble fibre, so less fruit should be eaten, particularly those containing small pips, such as strawberries and kiwi fruit, which can be irritating to the digestive tract. A bland diet, which includes skinned potatoes, steamed fish, poultry, soft vegetables such as zucchini, spinach, peas, butternut squash and wild yam, can be particularly beneficial.

Fish should constitute the main source of protein, because it contains anti-inflammatory omega-3 essential fatty acids and vitamin E, which is both an antioxidant and tissue-healing promoter. Foods rich in zinc are also vital for their healing properties. These foods include poultry, eggs and seafood (which also contains selenium, an antioxidant). Wholegrains, although they are a good source of zinc, should be omitted until all symptoms have abated.

Ulcerative colitis

The colon is the site of this painful condition, which causes ulcers to erupt. Typical symptoms include severe bloody diarrhoea and mucus in the faeces and acute pain.

Although fibre is needed, only one particular type is appropriate. We, as well as other nutritionists, recommend reducing insoluble fibre (found in foods such as sweetcorn, and high-starch vegetables such as carrots, turnip, parsnips and swede [rutabaga]), because it is difficult to digest if you have this condition. Also avoid wholegrains. Boiled white rice, which has a soothing effect on the digestive tract, can be eaten, especially if cooked with a little garlic. Nuts and seeds are too irritating, so avoid these.

All simple carbohydrates and sugars should also be eliminated from the diet – these include bread, biscuits, cakes, pies and also pasta. Wheat may be aggravating and may hinder the healing of the delicate intestinal tract. It is best to carefully check all foods for wheat content.

Sufferers find that eating small meals frequently throughout the day, rather than three main meals, is easier on the digestive tract. For the same reason, the evening meal should be kept light. Good foods to eat include those rich in soluble fibre such as fruits, green leafy vegetables and their juices, especially parsley, watercress, cabbage, collards and spinach. These will provide the body with fibre without being too abrasive.

Vitamin E is essential for the healing process, so eat plenty of avocados, kale and yams, which will help calm inflammation and soothe ulceration. Omega-3 essential fatty acids are anti-inflammatory, and can be found in oily fish such as salmon, tuna, herrings, sardines and mackerel. Sunflower and pumpkin seed oils will also help. However, buy cold-pressed oils and do not heat them.

Both Crohn's disease and ulcerative colitis are very serious diseases which can have life-threatening complications. Any nutritional manipulation should be carried out in combination with conventional medical care.

the immune system

The immune system is perhaps the most intricate of the body systems. It spends almost all its time dealing with potentially harmful invading particles. As you read this, the chances are that your immune system is doing battle with an army of pathogens (harmful tiny organisms, such as bacteria or viruses).

Pathogens are everywhere – in the air, on surfaces, in food and in water. They can be found on our bodies, lurking on skin, hair and under our nails. They also get inside us. If the immune system is not functioning at peak levels, these pathogens can precipitate an infection.

But how often do we think about looking after our immune system? Most people know that it is a good idea to take a vitamin C supplement and drink more orange juice when they have a cold, but that is about the extent of their knowledge. Although understanding exactly how the immune system operates is a lifetime's work, it is important to grasp the basics, so that you know how nutrition and lifestyle can help or hinder your immunity. Meanwhile, find out how good your immune system is by answering the questions in the quiz on page 82.

Basic defence

The body has some cunning defence systems to guard it against harm. The very first line of defence is the skin, which forms a barrier around us. Its surface is protected by sebum, an oily layer that inhibits the growth of some bacteria. Sweat glands within the skin also assist in fighting off tiny, potentially harmful microbes, by releasing perspiration to help wash them away from the skin's surface.

The tear ducts in our eyes help eliminate possible pathogenic bacterial invaders by producing extra fluid in an effort to flush away offending particles. Hayfever sufferers are acutely aware of this reaction during the summer months, when pollen counts are high and the eyes struggle to repel irritant grains of pollen with streaming tears.

The air that we breathe contains many malevolent particles, which the respiratory tract works to combat. The internal skin (epithelium) of the respiratory tract is lined with tiny, hair-like protrusions (cilia), which trap and collect foreign particles. The secretion of mucus increases in order to help trap pathogens – a substance called secretory immunoglobin A (sIgA), found in mucus, has the ability to neutralize would-be invaders.

LEFT Berry fruits are high in vitamin C and help to strengthen immunity.

Immune system quiz

How efficient is your immune system? Testing yourself with the following questions will give you an indication.

1 Do you often get colds, sniffles or flu?

2 If you have a cold, is it hard to get rid of?

3 Do you frequently feel stressed?

4 Do you suffer from depression or anxiety?

5 Are you allergic to any foods?

6 Do you use painkillers on a regular basis?

7 Do you suffer from hayfever?

8 Have you used antibiotics more than once in the last year?

9 Do you suffer from sore throats?

10 Do you drink alcohol more than three times a week?

11 Do you often get headaches?

- If you have answered 'yes' to three questions, your immune system may well need some support.
- If you have answered 'yes' to four questions, it is much more likely that your immune system requires attention.
- Answering 'yes' to five or more shows that your system is probably over-taxed.

The saliva in the mouth helps flush away microbes that are either airborne in origin, or have entered attached to food. When the saliva is swallowed, it mingles with gastric fluid in the stomach which contains a strong acid called hydrochloric acid (see pages 69–70). This destroys most of bacteria that has been ingested. Some bacteria, however, such as *Heliobacter pylori*, are not destroyed. If microbes do manage to get as far as our intestines, the beneficial flora (bacteria) living there will combat the invaders.

In short, the whole body has some protection on the outside and the inside. Sometimes, however, despite the body's best efforts, harmful invaders do break through the body's defence system and cause illness.

The immune force

So what does happens when we ingest or inhale a potentially harmful microbe or pathogen? The 'immune force' which protects us is rather like a naval fleet surrounding an island – the body. The

but they also have the ability to attract pathogens which, in turn, draws the attention of the white blood cells. Red blood cells have a short lifespan, and once they are no longer effective and are filtered out and broken down.

Some immune cells sail through the body on the lookout for foes, while others have set positions and attack enemies that happen to pass by.

fleet protects us from the outside world and is also responsible for detecting and clearing away debris and cells that are behaving unusually, such as cancerous cells. Commanders in strategic positions control individual craft and direct them into battle where required.

The fleet is made up of immune cells. Some of them sail through the body on the lookout for foes, while others have set positions and attack enemies that happen to pass by them. The wandering cells are known as macrophages, and have the ability to destroy and digest pathogens, a process that is known as phagocytosis (see page 84).

The immune cells are generally carried in the blood. There are two types of blood cell, red and white, and each has different tasks.

Red blood cells

These are the most plentiful immune cells in the body. They are synthesized in bone marrow, from where they are released into the bloodstream. The primary role of red blood cells is to carry and deliver oxygen around the body,

White blood cells

There are several types of white blood cell and their role is to defend the body. Certain white cells deal with parasitic and allergic reactions such as hayfever and asthma, while others cope with inflammation and infections.

The T-helper cell is an important white blood cell. When it senses the presence of a pathogen, it acts as an early-warning system, alerting the body's immune system defenders to launch an attack on the invader. In cases of HIV, it is these T-helper cells that are diminished, causing the immune system to fail to react to an invasion.

Complement and Interferon

Complement and interferon are also part of the immune navy. They resemble additional marine forces, which the navy can send for when it needs some back-up. They have specific targets and are called upon when other parts of the immune system recognize particular pathogens. Complement is specifically involved with the destruction of tumour cells and disarming some viruses, such as *herpes simplex*. Interferon is a substance that is secreted by most tissue as a means of self-defence, once it has been affected by a pathogen. It has antiviral properties and relies directly upon vitamin C and the mineral manganese: this is why additional vitamin C is so necessary during the treatment of colds and flu.

Tracking an infection

In order to see how the immune system functions, let's track the progress of an infection to see how it sets about causing illness.

Imagine you are sitting with friends in a café, enjoying breakfast. The person on the next table sneezes. Minute droplets are sprayed into the air at speeds up to 100mph (185 kph). They are, for only a few seconds, infectious. As luck would have it, you inhale. The infectious agent that caused your breakfast neighbour to sneeze has now found a new host – you.

Your immune system swings straight into action: first, your nose tries to trap and neutralize the pathogen. If this fails, the pathogen enters the body tissue, where it damages cells, releasing substances usually held within them, such as histamine. This is part of the process of inflammation, described in detail on pages 90-97. The release of histamine alerts white blood cells (see page 83), which travel to the affected tissue and begin their work of destroying the pathogen. Now the pathogen is damaged, and its own cells leak antigens, which attract the attention of the B-lymphocytes. These set about manufacturing 'nets' to trap and engulf the pathogen, effectively disarming it by making it visible to the macrophages, which come along and digest the invader.

During this process, you would probably experience a rise in temperature as your body resets its internal thermometer to disable the pathogen. You might have a sore throat, a blocked nose and headaches – all the classic symptoms of a cold.

But what of your companions at breakfast? Perhaps they were infected too, perhaps not. The strength (or weakness) of the immune system underlines our biochemical individuality. Someone whose immune system has been lowered by poor nutrition and immunosuppressors such as sugar and alcohol, may develop the cold, whereas someone with a strong immune system is likely to be relatively unaffected, because the mobilized immune fleet will deal with the infection promptly.

For each person, the pathogen remains the same, but the territory it encounters differs. We will now look at how best to provide your immune system with the nutrition that it requires.

Nutrition and the immune system

While the immune force is battling a cold virus, it it likely that other pathogens are trying to invade the body at the same time. The constant threat of infection puts the immune force under tremendous pressure, and we must help it by ensuring that it is supplied with all the nutrients necessary for peak fighting performance. Feeding the troops must be the highest priority.

nutrition know-how

For the perfect immune-boosting lunch, why not try the delicious sunrise pepper salad on page 138. This will provide ample vitamin C, together with magnesium, calcium and selenium.

Vitamin C

Vitamin C is perhaps the most important vitamin for the health of the immune system. It has potent antiviral properties, which is important because viruses, even when dormant, have been shown to undermine immunity. Its role as a support for interferon and complement has already been discussed (see page 83).

Vitamin C is also antibacterial: it detoxifies bacteria and prevents them from replicating. In addition, it is essential for the process of disarming and devouring invading pathogens, carried out by the immune cells, which stimulate the production of specific antibodies. This process is enhanced by the presence of zinc.

The important, positive effects that vitamin C has on immunity must not be underestimated. When the immune system is undermined, it is critically important to meet the increased need for this vital nutrient. When in good health, an adult needs 1000–3000mg per day of vitamin C. This requirement can double or treble when the immune system is compromised.

The body cannot manufacture its own vitamin C, so it must obtain an adequate supply each day through diet and nutritional supplements. Rich natural sources include kiwi fruit, strawberries, watermelon and sweet potatoes. If your diet contains plenty of fruit and vegetables, you should be getting enough vitamin C. However, if you drink a lot of alcohol, smoke, are under a lot of stress, or at a time when your immune system needs particular support, the vitamin C provided by food may require additional supplementation.

One way to gauge whether the body has reached its limit of vitamin C is the bowel tolerance test. If diarrhoea occurs, it indicates that the cells have been flooded with vitamin C, and the dose should be cut back by half.

Vitamin A

The immune system needs adequate vitamin A in order to function well, because it has potent antiviral properties. Plentiful amounts exist in red and yellow fruits and vegetables, such as carrots, peaches and pumpkin; also green vegetables such as broccoli. Plus it is found in hard cheese, eggs and liver. Pregnant women should not take vitamin A supplements, or eat liver, unless advised to do so by their doctor.

Vitamin B6

The white cells' ability to eat up offending pathogens is enhanced by this vitamin. Furthermore, the thymus gland requires good levels of B6. Food sources include brown rice, brewer's yeast and green vegetables.

Magnesium

This vital mineral is often lacking from the diet. In the context of immunity, magnesium is involved in the synthesis of complement (see page 83), and is essential in ensuring proper thymus function. Magnesium is also

nutrition know-how

If you have been using antibiotics, rebalance the gut bacteria by eating an unsweetened live bio yoghurt at least three times a week. These are available made from cow's, sheep's or goat's milk.

required for the formation of prostaglandins (hormone-like compounds found in all tissues) and for controlling histamine levels (see page 94). Magnesium is found in dark green vegetables, fish, soya beans, fresh nuts and seeds such as sesame and pumpkin seeds.

Calcium

Another vital mineral, calcium plays many roles in the immune system. Firstly, it is involved in the synthesis of the enzymes that T-cells use to

Selenium is involved in antibody synthesis. Without it, an immune cell cannot efficiently copy the cells that it produces in response to a repeated infection. Like many nutrients, selenium works best in combination with a vitamin, in this case vitamin E (see page 79).

Rich sources of selenium are liver, shellfish, onions, garlic, wholegrains and cereals (granolas) – although a certain amount can be derived from green vegetables.

Constant threat of infection puts the immune force under tremendous pressure. It must be supplied with all the nutrients necessary for peak fighting performance.

defeat pathogenic invaders. Like vitamin C, it is essential for enabling the white cells to digest and destroy certain viruses. Complement is also dependent on adequate calcium in the body. Although high levels of calcium are found in dairy products, these usually contain a lot of saturated fats which are considered to be pro-inflammatory and therefore detrimental to the immune system. It is better to get calcium from eggs and fish. Eating nuts, seeds and green vegetables provides a good balance of both calcium and magnesium.

Selenium

Selenium levels in crops and vegetables depend on the soil that they are grown in. Today, some areas of farmland have been shown to have particularly low levels of this trace mineral; consequently food grown there will be mineral-deficient, although it may look and taste perfect.

Iron

Iron can be both helpful and detrimental to the immune system. It plays an essential role in the production of all white blood cells, and is involved in the synthesis of antibodies. However, if too much iron is present, bacteria thrive. This is not to say that during an infection, iron-rich foods should be excluded from the diet. However, supplements containing iron should not be taken at this time.

The richest sources of iron are green vegetables, liver and wholegrain bread. It is also found in dried fruits and cereals (granolas).

Zinc

The thymus gland requires zinc to manufacture the T-cells that fight pathogens entering the body. Zinc is also needed to encourage the T-cells towards active maturity.

The top ten vegetables for the immune system

When you have an infection, make sure that you eat lots of raw and lightly steamed vegetables, because they help the immune system to fight pathogens. The vegetables below are ideal, as they contain high levels of antioxidants to help combat damage by free radicals. In addition, they have strong antiviral, antibacterial and anti-fungal properties, as well as being natural antibiotics.

To ensure that you also get adequate carbohydrate and protein, plan meals to include lentils, wholegrain bread and brown rice, which are also good sources of minerals to boost the immune system.

Manganese

This trace mineral is required for interferon production (see page 83). The body often lacks an adequate amount of it. Its jobs are to form bone and cartilage, and control glucose metabolism. Signs that one is low in manganese include poor balance, confusion and sore knees. Good sources are wholegrain cereals (granolas), pulses (legumes), green vegetables, wheatgerm, rice bran, tea, nuts, ginger and cloves. Factors that hinder absorption of manganese include tea, coffee, smoking and high doses of iron and zinc.

Immune Inhibitors

We have seen which nutrients boost and support the immune system, so we should also look at which nutritional and other influences hinder the workings of our vital protection force.

Sugar

Sugar, in any form, inhibits the ability of the white cells that digest pathogens, for up to five hours after eating it. A sugary cereal (granola) at breakfast, followed by sweet snacks, soft drinks and sweet tea or coffee throughout the day,

Improving immunity – power eating

To boost your immune system, choose at least five fruits and vegetables from the list below for every day of the week.

Monday
Blackcurrants, grapefruit, canteloupe, apple, carrots, beetroot, celery, kale.

Friday
Blueberries, peach, papaya, cauliflower, coconut, potatoes, spinach.

Tuesday
Nectarine, orange, lemon and lime, brocolli, fennel, squash and pumpkin.

Saturday
Strawberries, blackcurrants, cranberries, prunes, asparagus, celeriac, palm hearts, collards.

Wednesday
Satsumas, clementines, mango, Brussels sprouts, onions, tomato, sweet potato.

Sunday
Raspberries, cranberries, cherries, pineapple, avocade. radish, turnip.

Thursday
Apricots, dates, figs, cabbage, garlic, nettles, watercress.

followed by an instant meal high in hidden sugars, can permanently suppress your immune system. Give it up. It has no nutritional value, rots your teeth and makes you put on weight.

Alcohol

As a simple sugar, alcohol has the same effect. Even if your immune system is in good working order, supported by a diet high in nutrients, alcohol can inhibit the beneficial activity of the immune cells. Although it is true that a glass of red wine contains important antioxidants, there is a balance to be struck. One glass a day has been shown to have a positive overall effect on health (particularly the heart), but if you drink more, the law of diminishing returns applies.

Caffeine

Coffee, tea and fizzy drinks all contain caffeine and inhibit the absorption of vital nutrients, in addition to directly suppressing the immune system. Green tea, however, has been found to stimulate immune function, and should become a regular substitute for the caffeinated black Chinese version. Mineral water helps to clear toxins from the body, lessening the immune system's daily struggle.

Stress

Stress suppresses the production of white blood cells and can lead to the inhibition of the thymus gland. The lymphatic cells in the thymus, and the lymph nodes throughout the body disintegrate, reducing the protection offered by these important parts of the immune system. For more on stress and the immune system, see page 58. To learn more on the lymphatic system, see pages 104–119 on heart and circulation.

Bereavement

Losing someone close to you has a profound effect on the immune system. This should never be underestimated, and it is often found that old health problems will come to the fore within a few months of a personal loss. Sometimes these conditions present themselves in an even more severe form than when they first occurred. If you are concerned, see your doctor for a check-up to ascertain whether or not symptoms are new or a recurrence 'in sympathy'.

Bereavement does not just apply to the death of a relative or friend. There are other types of loss, such as leaving an old family home, or the breakdown of a relationship. Changing career may also have a physiological effect on the immune system.

Antibiotics

The immune system is closely associated with the health of the gut. The gut, or colon, contains millions of bacteria, some of which are considered 'friendly' and others which are not. The colon has a natural balance of bacteria, yet this balance is sensitive and can easily be upset, both by an excess of simple sugars and also by taking antibiotics. Doctors are nowadays trying to prescribe fewer antibiotics, because it is thought that our over-reliance on them is endangering the population's future ability to fight disease.

nutrition know-how
To make an immune-boosting power juice, blend 85 g (3 oz) each of strawberries, raspberries and blackcurrants together with 1/3 litre (1/2 pt) soya milk and one teaspoon of sesame seeds.

Many bacteria produce natural antibiotics which act against viruses, bacteria and fungal infections. If medicinal antibiotics are taken, they damage some of these friendly bacteria, along with the 'target' bacteria.

The yeast *Candida albicans*, which lives in all of us (usually quite happily) can get out of control and proliferate. In so doing, it inhibits immune action by decreasing the production of white blood cells. Frequent use of antibiotics can encourage an overgrowth of *Candida albicans*, but it can be tamed by a strict diet that excludes all sugars and includes natural antibiotics and anti-fungals such as garlic and onions.

People who have a history of antibiotic use should follow a regime that will recolonize the gut with friendly bacteria. We have seen the immune system respond very well to this treatment. We advise supplementing with 'probiotics' in the form of live, unsweetened bio yoghurt, rich in *Lactobacillus acidophilus* and *Bifidobacteria*. It should be eaten three times a week. If preferred, supplements of these probiotics are available.

inflammation

Inflammation is a reaction to injury, infection, or an aggravating substance. Most people view an attack of inflammation, with its associated pain, swelling and redness, as unpleasant and inconvenient. However, it is actually a very positive and welcome action, necessary for the body to repair itself.

The immune system is the body's protector, swinging into action whenever it is needed. It harnesses its resources to fight off invaders such as bacteria and viruses, or to help recovery from injury and disease, or to create a reaction to an outside stimulant or aggravating factor – and for the human body, one of the most powerful of these is food. The immune system tackles the problems by providing a series of responses, inflammation being one of them.

There is a vast amount of evidence to show that our diet has a direct relationship with the immune system's ability to function well. For example, a diet rich in fruit, vegetables, essential fatty acids and wholegrains can help control the inflammation response; while a poor diet consisting predominantly of convenience foods, red meat and dairy products can lead to unnecessary inflammation.

Certain foods are noted for their anti-inflammatory properties, such as strawberries and lentils. Other foods, such as tomatoes and potatoes, are thought to promote inflammation.

Types of inflammation

There are two types of inflammation: acute and chronic. Acute inflammation occurs as the body's response to trauma (injury), irritation, infection or an allergen (ranging from chemicals to food). Chronic inflammation is a long-term problem. Contributory factors include overuse of a particular part of the body, general wear and tear, and getting older.

The primary signs of acute inflammation are pain, swelling, redness and heat. These are caused by blood vessels dilating around the affected area, bringing immune mediators (substances involved in the inflammation process) to dispense or disperse the damaged tissue or bacteria. This is the first part of the process of healing. However, if healing does not occur for any reason, chronic inflammation follows, caused by the immune system becoming either overstimulated, overactive or failing to switch off – or any combination of the three. An example of this is systemic lupus, an autoimmune condition that can affect many organs of the body (see page 101).

LEFT Asparagus is a liver tonic and helps reduce inflammation.

The inflammation process

Inflammation is a common occurrence. Imagine what happens if we cut or knock a finger: the area becomes red and swollen, sometimes accompanied by pain, and this may lead to temporary loss of function. This reaction is the same wherever it occurs in the body, and from whatever the cause – whether the injury is a physical blow, an internal stress or an irritant.

Most people react to inflammation by reaching for an anti-inflammatory painkiller. In fact, so many of us do this that non-prescription painkillers have become the world's biggest-selling drugs. But while inflammation may be unpleasant, it is actually a positive sign that the immune system is functioning well.

So, instead of reaching into the medicine cabinet, we should recognize that the process of inflammation is a vital function of the immune system and that when it occurs, it is only our natural defences being mobilized to deal with the injury, however small. Given a chance, the body has the ability to heal itself.

The three stages of inflammation

The process of inflammation is a fascinating combined effort by the skin, blood and immune cells to repair, replace and renew the damaged tissue. It takes place in three stages.

The first stage happens when the body rushes into action as soon as any part it is affected. Immediately, the blood vessels around the injured area dilate to allow more blood to flow to the site, bringing with it the necessary nutrients and immune cells to repair and seal off the injury.

During the second stage, the immune defence team homes in on any bacteria that are present. Neutrophil cells congregate in the affected tissue, ready to engulf the bacteria completely and digest it. This amazing response, called phagocytosis, involves the cells actually changing shape – they grow tiny arms (pseudopods) that wrap around the foreign bacteria, completely overwhelming it. The cells then release chemicals that destroy the offending microbe. The cells also carry antioxidants to protect themselves from potential damage by free radicals.

Characteristics of inflammation

Redness

Pain

Swelling

Heat

Loss of function

What's in a name?

In simple terms, 'itis' means 'inflamed', and is tacked on to various other words to describe problems in that area. For example, 'arthritis' describes joint inflammation ('arthro' means 'joints'). 'Dermatitis' is inflammation of the skin ('derma' means 'skin').

An 'itis' isn't the only form of inflammation. Many other conditions such as asthma, Crohn's disease (see page 78) and psoriasis are also linked to the inflammation response.

It is not just the bacteria that can get eaten in the phagocytosis process. Damaged and dead cells are also removed in the same way. This leads to the third stage, when the inflamed site is made into a self-contained area, cut off from the surrounding tissue. The affected area is likely to feel sensitive, sometimes painful, and it often throbs. This forces us to rest the damaged part. Histamine is released from the immune cells (mast cells), increasing the permeability of blood vessels. This allows toxins and waste products to flow away more efficiently.

Give me fever

The most dramatic reaction in the inflammation repertoire is fever. This occurs when there is a challenging infection that requires the immune force to be at its most potent. Fevers can be alarming, but understanding exactly what is happening can help dispel the fear. Fever creates a series of individual reactions in the body, all of which work together to fight off the cause of the fever. These responses, and their causes, are shown in the box on page 94.

Body temperature shoots up during a fever, peaking as the battle against the infection reaches its climax. But we may feel cold and shivery, ensuring that we wrap up warmly or – better still – retire to bed. The body appears to shut down. We feel weak, our senses are dulled, speech becomes difficult, food seems unappetizing and we may feel separated from the world around us. The body is telling us that it needs uninterrupted rest to repair itself. These symptoms may last for as long as three days – roughly as long as it takes the immune system to do its magical rejuvenation work.

During this shut-down time, the body is battling the invading bacteria without distraction. Bacteria survive and flourish at 98.6°F (37°C) – which is normal body temperature. While we are running a temperature, bacteria cannot thrive and their ability to reproduce is reduced. The cells that engulf them increase, called up from elsewhere in the body. As the body's temperature continues to rise, the balance of power tips in our favour: now there are fewer bacteria and an increased number of white blood cells. It is at this point that the battle has been won. The fever breaks.

Why fever is good for you

A fever can be quite dramatic and worrying for the onlooker as well as for the person experiencing the battle raging inside the body. Modern medicine has developed methods to bring down fever; however interrupting a fever also disrupts the natural process of defence and is often the cause of longer and repeated bouts of infection. This is frequently seen in children's ear, nose and throat infections.

This is not to say that fever should be left unchecked. In adults it is not uncommon to see a fever temperature of up to 40°C (104°F). Short periods of such high fever are usually safe, but ensure that your doctor is made aware of the condition.

nutrition know-how

Vitamin C can flush out toxins and lower temperature. Encourage a feverish child to sip diluted orange juice throughout the day.

Warning. In children, the fever response is more frequent and should never be ignored. Seek medical advice if your child's temperature is persistent or is accompanied by drowsiness, delirium, repeated vomiting or severe pain. Beware of a high fever and a skin rash that does not disappear when pressed – this could indicate meningitis and requires urgent medical help. High fever can also cause epileptic fits and may need to be controlled by cooling measures.

Causes of inflammation

A variety of triggers lead to inflammation, including environmental, metabolic, nutritional, structural, digestive, infectious or drug-induced factors. Five substances respond to these influences: histamine, kinins, prostaglandins, leukotrienes and complement. Some are helpful, some are not. Good nutritional sources to promote or combat these five substances are listed in the chart on page 96.

Histamine

This substance is derived from the mast cells and is made from histadine, an amino acid. Histamine has many effects on the body, some of which are involved in the immune process. It contracts the smooth muscles and encourages the dilation of blood vessels. It is released in large amounts after the skin has been damaged, as seen when a weal develops. Some people produce more histamine than others. Hayfever sufferers are typically high histamine producers.

To counter some of the effects of inflammation, it is important to reduce the production of histamine. This can be achieved without resorting to over-the-counter antihistamine preparations, simply by including some basic nutrients in your daily diet, as outlined in the chart on page 96. Taking antihistamines can have a negative effect on the body as they need to be detoxified by the liver, causing unnecessary stress. This is in turn makes the liver less

The body's reaction to fever

Response	Reason
Raised temperature	Reduces the activity of bacteria that thrive at normal body temperature.
Faster breathing	Increases flow of oxygen throughout the body.
Faster heart rate	Pumps more blood to the affected area, to deliver essential nutrients for healing and repair.
Sweating	Speeds up the elimination of toxins through the skin and regulates temperature.

effective at detoxifying natural histamine, creating a need for antihistamines – and so the cycle continues!

Kinins

Kinins are polypeptides ('poly' means 'many'; 'peptide' means 'protein molecule'). Like histamine, they are derived from amino acids. Unlike other parts of the immune force, however, kinins are not found circulating in the blood: they are produced only in response to tissue damage or if there is a change in body temperature, such as a fever.

The body maintains a strict balance between acidity and alkalinity and employs buffering systems to maintain it. Quinines are released into the blood if this delicate acid/alkaline balance (the pH) is altered in response to a breakdown of tissue caused by high acidity. For example, stress will encourage a highly acid state in the body, as will a high-protein diet.

DIY test for histamine levels

To give you an indication of your histamine levels, do this simple test. Roll up your sleeve and lightly scratch the inside of your forearm from wrist to elbow. Within a minute or less, a red mark will appear where you have scratched. This is histamine being called to the site of trauma to help heal it. The greater the intensity of redness and possible swelling, the higher your histamine levels.

Prostaglandins

Prostaglandins are very short-lived substances that act like hormones. They affect the tissue immediately around them and cause the constriction of smooth muscles. Prostaglandins are produced from essential fatty acids, which must be obtained from the diet. There are three different types of prostaglandin: Pg-1, Pg-2 and Pg-3.

Pg-1 and Pg-3 are very important to the body. They are not only anti-inflammatory, but help to reduce cholesterol, lower blood pressure and prevent blood clotting as well. They also help raise high-density lipoprotein (HDL) levels in the body to protect against heart disease.

Pg-2 is a 'bad' prostaglandin, promoting inflammation. It also raises cholesterol and blood pressure, encourages blood clotting and lowers HDL levels. Avoid Pg-2 foods, such as animal and dairy products, which are rich in saturated fats.

Leukotrienes

Less is known about leukotrienes than of some of the other mediators of inflammation. They are related to prostaglandins and generated from arachidonic acid. Leukotrienes play a role in promoting the inflammatory response, especially allergic responses.

Complement

Complement is a protein found in the blood and is usually inactive. There are about ten different types of complement and, when activated, they improve, or complement, the immune system,

Nutrients to reduce inflammation caused by various substances

	Nutrients
To counter histamine	• Blackcurrants, kiwi fruit, cherries and rosehips are all rich sources of vitamin C, a natural antihistamine. Ideally, they should be taken with bioflavanoids to enhance absorption of the vitamin. • Quercetin protects the white blood cells from reacting to excess histamine and is considered a potent anti-inflammatory agent. Good food sources include blue-green algae such as spirulina, kelp and green magma. • Ginger root is another natural antihistamine and can be used either raw or cooked. (See pages 130-155.) • B vitamins such as biotin, choline and inositol all support the liver, which detoxifies circulating histamine. Good food sources include buckwheat, brown rice, calf's liver, chicken, eggs, lentils, oats and sunflower seeds. • Methionine is an essential amino acid required for optimal liver detoxification. Good food sources include eggs, fish, meat and poultry. • Silymarin also supports liver function. It is found in the herb milk thistle.
To beat kinins	• Eating a diet rich in vegetables and fruits will lower kinin levels. • Cranberry juice is highly alkaline and so helps to rebalance the body if it is too acidic. • High-protein foods such as chicken, nuts tofu, fish and pulses (legumes) are all acid-promoting. • Salt, soya sauce, vinegar and other condiments are highly acid-producing.
Anti-prostaglandins	• Pineapple contains bromelain, which blocks pro-inflammatory prostaglandins, as well as increasing anti-inflammatory prostaglandins. • Ginger inhibits pro-inflammatory prostaglandins. • The enzymes that ensure successful production of pro-inflammatory prostaglandins require vitamins C, B3, B6 and biotin as well as the minerals magnesium and zinc.
Anti-leukotrienes	• Quercetin prevents the release of leukotrienes. The most concentrated source of quercetin can be found in the outer folds of onions. It is also more abundant in red onions than other onions. • Turmeric spice contains curcumin: this reduces pro-inflammatory leukotriene production. • All animal products contain arginine, an amino acid that is thought to inhibit the action of leukotrienes.
To inhibit complement activation	• Vitamins A, C and E, and the minerals selenium and zinc are all antioxidants, which help to quell free radicals. Yellow, red and orange fruits and vegetables such as peaches, peppers and tomatoes are rich in vitamin A. High levels of vitamin C are found in berries, potatoes and kiwi fruit. Selenium is found is seafood and sesame seeds, while zinc can be obtained from pumpkin seeds and oysters.

hence their name. They serve to dilate arterioles, which are tiny arteries serving the blood capillaries. Complement is also involved in the release of histamine from the mast cells, further exacerbating inflammation.

Hyperimmunity
– an immune system out of control

We can see that inflammation is a vital and efficient way for the body to repair itself, so why and how does the inflammatory process become damaging? There are four reasons why the immune system can become overstimulated.

1 The immune system is frequently or constantly challenged.

Examples of challenges include food intolerances, environmental stresses such as toxic chemicals and pollution, infections, vaccinations, excessive alcohol, nicotine, 'recreational' drugs, eating a diet high in saturated fats, and relying too much on convenience foods.

2 There can be an over-firing of the normal inflammatory response.

This can be attributed to deficiencies of nutrients, specifically the antioxidants and bioflavanoids responsible for neutralizing damaging free radicals.

3 The immune system fails to shut down once the inflammation has fulfilled its function.

This leads to autoimmunity, a condition in which the body fails to recognize the difference between its own cells and foreign matter. It reaches a state of confusion (this is often precipitated by exhaustion, viruses, bacterial infections, and sometimes – possibly – vaccinations), where it in effect turns against itself and attacks its own cells, rather than defending them from outside invaders.

nutrition know-how
To help relieve cystitis, drink at least three glasses of unsweetened cranberry juice each day until symptoms disappear. Cranberry juice is highly alkaline, which balances the acidity of the inflamed bladder.

4 The immune force may be called into action for an inappropriate reason.

This can occur because of an overactive immune system, or as a result of damage to the cells of an organ (an example of this is rheumatoid arthritis). Foods to help combat the debilitating conditions of rheumatoid arthritis and osteoarthritis are listed in the chart on page 99.

Endocrine involvement

The endocrine glands, such as the thyroid, pancreas and ovaries, may play a part in hyperimmunity. This happens when a person has been subjected to physical trauma, endured prolonged stress or is recovering from a long-term illness. Because the immune system is in overdrive, this puts added stress on the adrenals glands, causing hormonal imblance. This can cause some of the body's cells to start attacking themselves. An example of this is Grave's Disease and Type II (Maturity Onset) diabetes.

allergens and inflammatory conditions

The connection between food allergies and inflammation is a strong one. Familiar reactions to allergens are sneezing, headaches, fluid retention or bloating. To these we must add inflammation, particularly of the joints, and most especially that of arthritic conditions.

In this section, we'll look at a range of common illnesses with inflammation as a symptom, and provide dietary advice for combating them. But first, here's a little bit more about how a food allergy and the digestive system do battle with each other.

Attack that stranger!

The food allergy process starts at the gut lining, which is as thin as the skin of the eyelid. Certain substances, such as vitamins and minerals, are able to cross the lining and get into the bloodstream. Sometimes, though, the gut lining allows partially digested food (that still has to be broken down completely by the digestive system) to cross over into the bloodstream. This condition is known as a leaky gut, or, to give it its proper name, increased intestinal permeability. Read more about it on page 71.

Not recognizing the food molecules in the bloodstream, the white blood cells in the immune force launch an attack. In order for the invading food type to be identified and dealt with in the future, the immune system manufactures antibodies to use against the substance, should it ever be detected in the bloodstream again. If the gut is permeable, an intolerant response is more likely to recur. This results in inflammation affecting vulnerable areas, such as the joints and cartilage.

Food culprits

Sometimes it is a food itself that causes a direct reaction. The most common allergens in Europe are wheat, dairy products and citrus fruits. In the United States, corn is frequently used in breads and baked goods, and so it is a more common allergen than wheat. If you suspect a food allergy, work with a nutrition consultant to establish what you are allergic to. You can then devise an eating plan that avoids these foods.

Inflammatory conditions
Osteoarthritis and rheumatoid arthritis

When people talk of arthritis, they seldom realize that there are many different forms of this debilitating joint condition. However, the two most common types are rheumatoid arthritis and osteoarthritis. There are significant differences between the two; there are also specific nutrients that will combat the diseases (see the boxes on page 99). Sufferers should attempt to follow the anti-inflammatory treatment plan on page 103.

The differences between osteoarthritis and rheumatoid arthritis

Osteoarthritis	Rheumatoid arthritis
• Structural and degenerative effects. • May be caused by joint strain or injury. • Calcium imbalance is possible. • Onset usually in middle age. • Affects 90 per cent of the population. • Typically attacks hips, knees and ankles. • Pain or stiffness is experienced in affected joints. • Occurs in a gradual, progressive manner.	• Systemic, viral or bacterial cause. A blood test will show the presence of autoimmune rheumatoid factor. • Allergies, intolerances, nutrient deficiencies or free radicals may be the cause. • Onset usually after the age of 30. Sometimes affects children. Afflicts three times as many women as men. • Typically found in the fingers, wrists, knees and ankles. • Inflammation, redness, swelling and fluid retention in the affected area. • Occurs for sporadic, intermittent periods when it flares up, then goes into remission.

Nutrients required to combat arthritis

Follow the nutritional advice below, as well as the guidelines given in the anti-inflammatory treatment plan (page 103).

Osteoarthritis	Rheumatoid arthritis
• Chondroitin sulphate, available as a mineral supplement, for regeneration of bones, ligaments and cartilage. • Calcium and magnesium for bone formation. Magnesium is essential for the reabsorption of calcium. Found in dark green leafy vegetables, cheese, nuts and seeds. • Manganese, a co-factor for bone reabsorption. Found in ginger, avocados, buckwheat and spinach. • Boron and silica, trace minerals are found in kelp, seaweed and other sea vegetables. • Vitamin D, essential for the reabsorption of calcium. Found in fish oils, or made by the body after exposure to direct sunlight.	• Essential fatty acids involved in Pg-1 and Pg-3 anti-inflammatory pathways. Found in nuts, seeds and their oils and oily fish such as salmon and mackerel. • Biotin and vitamin B3, co-factors for anti-inflammatory essential fatty acids pathways. Found in wholegrains, lentils, liver, tuna, soya and sunflower seeds. • Chromium, involved in insulin-related inflammation. Found in brewer's yeast, chicken, oysters and grains.

Ankylosing spondylitis

Ankylosing spondylitis is an arthritic condition, although it tends to be less well documented than other types of arthritis. Its name describes inflammation of the joints of the spine.

The disease is most common in young and middle-aged men, affecting the points at which ligaments and tendons attach to the joint bones. It usually starts where the pelvis and spine meet (the sacro-iliac joint). Classic symptoms include a rigid spine and difficulty in holding the head up when walking.

Generally, ankylosing spondylitis first affects the lower back, giving rise to symptoms of lower back pain and stiffness. In extreme cases that are left untreated, the vertebrae can fuse together, causing discomfort and pain, and severely restricting movement and mobility.

The guidelines given in the anti-inflammatory treatment plan on page 103 will certainly offer some relief and, in many cases, may help reverse the early damage of ankylosing spondylitis. However, we recommend consulting a nutrition consultant or health practitioner, as well as a physiotherapist, to devise essential exercises to help loosen the area.

Fibromyalgia

This rheumatic disorder is characterized by chronic aching muscles with no obvious physical cause, often described by sufferers as shooting or burning pain. Fibromyalgia afflicts the lower back, neck, shoulders, thighs and upper chest, although other areas may be affected as well. The pain is often greater in the mornings. Other symptoms include stiffness, swelling, fatigue and numbness. Sleep disorders are common and patients often suffer from chronic fatigue.

The presence of 'tender points' – nine specific points, particularly sensitive to pressure – is a significant indicator of fibromyalgia. These nine points are as follows:

- Lower vertebrae of the neck.
- Second rib joint.
- Upper part of the thighbone.
- Middle of the knee joint.
- Muscles at the base of the skull.
- Neck and upper back muscles.
- Mid-back muscles.
- Side of elbow.
- Outer and upper muscles of the buttocks.

Symptoms of fibromyalgia are more common in women than men and begin in early adulthood. They become more intense with age, if left untreated. In many cases, symptoms clear up very quickly by themselves, but tend to return unless treatment is maintained. Following the guidelines given in the anti-inflammatory treatment plan (page 103) offers assistance by reducing muscle inflammation.

Multiple sclerosis

MS is an inflammation of the protective fatty layer surrounding the nerve cells, known as the myelin sheath. As the inflammation advances, the myelin sheath breaks down and is replaced by scar tissue, rendering the enclosed nerve ineffective. In its advanced stages, the disease can have devastating effects on a person's ability to move, speak and care for themselves.

The importance of anti-inflammatory essential fatty acids contained in fish, nuts and seeds cannot be overestimated, and pro-inflammatory foods should be completely avoided. There is much research that supports the use of dietary manipulation to relieve the painful symptoms of MS. Follow the guidelines given in the anti-inflammatory treatment plan (page 103).

Bronchitis and asthma

These two conditions are closely linked, and both are classified as inflammatory. Bronchitis is inflammation of the bronchial tubes; asthma describes difficulty in breathing due to inflammation of the bronchial tubes, coupled with an excessive production of mucus.

There are two categories of bronchitis. Acute bronchitis is often caused by a viral infection (usually of the respiratory tract) such as flu or the common cold. Chronic bronchitis is usually related to frequent irritation of the bronchial tubes, and can be caused by exposure to toxins, chemicals or cigarette smoke.

For asthma sufferers there are many possible villains that can set off an attack, ranging from environmental influences such as chemicals, feathers or food additives, to anxiety or even low blood sugar. All can result in the muscles that surround the bronchi becoming irritated and inflamed, thereby reducing the air flow to and from the lungs and leaving the asthmatic gasping for air.

Both conditions can be greatly helped by the guidelines given in the anti-inflammatory treatment plan on page 103. While this approach may not address all the causes, it should help alleviate many of the symptoms. In all cases, seek the advice of a nutrition consultant or health practitioner to identify and eliminate the allergens.

Lupus

Lupus is an autoimmune disease occurring when the body fails to recognize self and non-self, and so attacks its own tissues. It can be systemic (affecting the whole body: systems and organs). Some sufferers develop an unusual rash on their cheeks, which has been likened to the markings on a wolf. This gives the disease its name – 'lupus' is Latin for 'wolf'.

There are two types of lupus, both of which can differ in their severity. The less serious type, known as discoid lupus erythematosus (DLE), causes small lesions to form on the skin, leaving scars when they disappear. Systemic lupus erythematosus (SLE) is more serious, because it can affect far more than the skin. In its early stages, it is similar to arthritis, as inflammation of the joints and hands is not uncommon. A fever often accompanies these initial symptoms; many people go on to develop inflammation of the kidneys (nephritis) or other organs.

Following the guidelines given in the anti-inflammatory treatment plan (page103) may offer some relief, but it is essential to consult a doctor in the first instance.

Tendonitis and bursitis

Tendinitis is inflammation of the tendons, while bursitis is the inflammation of the bursae – fluid-filled cushions that lubricate the joints, reducing friction. Both conditions usually follow some form of trauma, for example sudden pressure or strain. Repeated movements can also lead to bursitis – housemaid's knee and frozen shoulder are both examples of it.

The two conditions are both inflammatory and often difficult to tell apart. Bursitis is usually associated with painful swelling and an accumulation of fluid, while the inflammation of tendonitis is not so obvious and is less severe. Bursitis is typically characterized by a dull ache that becomes more acute with movement; a sharp pain is more common with tendinitis.

As a basis for improving both conditions, follow the guidelines given in the anti-inflammatory treatment plan on page 103.

Gout

Gout is sometimes called crystal arthritis, as it caused by excess uric acid in the blood, tissues and urine. Uric acid is a substance that the body produces and excretes in the urine, via the kidneys.

nutrition know-how
The flavanols and high alkaline content of cherry juice are effective neutralizers of uric acid. Drink a glass daily to help relieve the pain of gout.

Uric acid can crystallize into needle-shaped crystals which 'jab' at the spaces in between joints, causing pain. Gout is often found in the big toe as well as the knees and ankles. A blood test can confirm whether uric acid levels in the blood are higher than normal.

Symptoms are similar to those of the other types of arthritis, in that the affected areas become painful and inflamed.

Gout used to be associated with too much high living and the consumption of rich food (because of the link between such foods and uric acid production). However, we now know that certain foods contain a substance called purine, which leads to excessive uric acid production. Purine-rich foods include meat, foods high in saturated fats, anchovies, herring, mackerel, sardines, scallops, liver, kidneys, sweetbreads and fish roe. These should all be avoided if you have a tendency to gout.

Foods low in purine include rice, millet, avocados, green vegetables, goat's milk, goat's yoghurt, eggs and non-citrus fruits.

Hayfever

Hayfever is an allergy to airborne particles, and it is a good example of how the inflammatory response operates in the air passages.

When a hayfever sufferer inhales airborne pollen, it causes the release of histamine as soon as the allergen makes contact with the lungs. Histamine is an inflammatory trigger (see page 94). It's not just pollen that causes hayfever House dust mites, animal hair, feathers or chemicals can start similar reactions.

The mast cells release histamine to encourage the expulsion of the pollen or other allergen – in other words they make us sneeze! Taking an antihistamine can reduce the response, and therefore the symptoms, but, at the same time, it may suppress the immune system. As antihistamines are chemicals, they require breaking down by a liver already taxed by the presence of excess natural histamine. The cycle needs to be broken.

If you decide to take nutritional supplements, start before the hayfever season, to give your body time to accumulate immunity as well as high levels of the various nutrients.

We do acknowledge that many people will need to take some sort of medication. Whilst antihistamines can be effective, please be aware of the histamine/liver connection and stick to the stated dose. Many people prefer a hayfever 'jab'. This lowers histamine release and is a good way of acquiring protection for a month or so. But it also affects general immunity, leaving you more prone to colds and other infections and is not generally recommended by the medical profession.

Eat foods that are rich in the anti-inflammatory vitamins A, B, and C, calcium, bioflavanoids, quercetin, methionine, and co-enzyme Q10.

Your natural anti-inflammatory treatment plan

- Avoid foods such as citrus fruits, wheat, eggs, shellfish, dairy products and chocolate. Much allergy-related inflammation is triggered by these foods.

- Don't eat foods from the nightshade family, which in cludes potatoes, tomatoes, peppers, aubergine (eggplant), Cape gooseberries, rhubarb and zucchini.

- Choose foods rich in vitamin A, found in red and yellow fruits and vegetables such as plums, peaches, pumpkin, squash and beetroot.

- Pick foods rich in vitamin C, such as strawberries, kiwi fruit and sweet potatoes.

- Eat foods containing bioflavanoids, which support vitamin C production. They are found in yellow and green vegetables such as squash, broccoli, kale, and dark berries such as blackcurrants.

- Avocados, sesame seeds, pumpkin seeds and sunflower seeds are rich in vitamin E, which is helpful for calming inflammation.

- Quercetin is a potent anti-inflammatory because it slows down histamine release. Quercetin is found in onions and kelp.

- Methionine is an amino acid found in protein foods. It binds to the excess histamine, making reactions less severe. Grade-A proteins include tuna, mackerel, herring, sardines, salmon, chicken and tofu.

- Bromelain is one of the most powerful anti-inflammatories, and is found in pineapples and nuts.

- Naringin, found in oranges and in the pith of grapefruit (particularly pink) is a helpful anti-inflammatory.

the heart and circulation

Research shows that the heart is capable of recovering from damage. As heart disease is one of the most common causes of death, making changes to diet and lifestyle are worthwhile. This hard-working muscle pumps around 17,600 pints (10,000 litres) of blood around the body every day.

The early stages of arterial disease carry few symptoms. In fact, most sufferers are unaware of any problems until they experience a heart attack or a stroke. Despite this, heart disease is the second biggest cause of death in the United Kingdom, accounting for nearly 170,000 deaths each year. Approximately one in three men and one in four women die from the disease. In the United States, heart disease accounts for more than one million deaths annually. And most heart problems can be avoided – or improved significantly – through diet.

The driving force of the cardiovascular system is the heart, which pumps blood around the body through an intricate series of veins and arteries. Essentially, the heart is a powerful muscle which requires nutrients of its own to carry out its job. The blood acts as a carrier, delivering fresh oxygen (and nutrients) to all the tissues, muscles and cells throughout the body.

Branching off the larger vessels of the heart are tiny blood capillaries that diffuse oxygen into the cells and remove waste products. The blood takes the waste products and disposes of them through the kidneys, liver and lungs. Back in the lungs, the blood is refreshed with oxygen and the cycle takes place all over again.

The veins and arteries that service the heart have different functions. Arteries transport newly oxygenated blood away from the heart; veins transport deoxygenated blood towards the heart. It may be easier to understand this if we imagine the blood as a conveyor belt running through the body, on to which gases are loaded, delivered, reloaded and exchanged at the appropriate point.

The lymphatic system

The lymphatic system is a completely closed and separate system to that of the arteries and veins, but it is an integral part of the whole circulation system. The fluid that runs through its arterial-type system, with one-way valves to prevent backflow, is called lymph. Its purpose is to carry away toxins from the arteries and veins. The lymphatic system is actually part of the immune system, filtering potentially harmful substances

LEFT Vitamin C is a potent guard against heart disease. Kiwi fruit is full of it.

and detoxifying them. The lymph passes through lymph glands, which are large collecting areas that trap circulating bacteria and viruses and prevent them from running riot throughout the body. The glands contain and form lymphocytes, a type of white blood cell. The T-lymphocytes are involved in attacking invading organisms. The lymph glands are found all over the body: under the arms, in the groin, and under the jawbone in particular. This explains the 'swollen glands' we experience when we have a bacterial infection – it is the body's immune system dealing with it.

exercise, further raising their risk of being affected by cardiovascular complications. Carrying excess weight around puts a strain on all the body organs, especially the heart, which has to pump harder. As fat accumulates in the body, it also increases in the arteries.

Age

The risk of coronary heart disease rises with age, because damage to the arteries accumulates over the years and blood pressure rises accordingly, presenting a risk factor.

Just ten years after stopping smoking, the likelihood of cardiovascular complications will have reduced to almost the same as that of someone who has never smoked.

Factors contributing to heart disease

Having examined how the heart works, let's look at the factors that can contribute to coronary heart disease.

Gender

Men suffer more coronary heart disease than women. As yet, we do not know why this is. However, once women reach the menopause and no longer have the protective female hormone oestrogen, their rate of disease roughly matches that of men.

Excess weight

Being overweight is known to increase blood pressure and affect the sensitive ratio of 'bad' cholesterol (low-density lipoproteins, or LDL) to 'good' cholesterol (high-density lipoproteins, or HDL). Obese people are often unable to

Trans fats intake

A high intake of trans fats, derived from saturated fats found in animal products, increases the risk of coronary heart disease. Many products, such as margarine, cakes and biscuits, contain it. In the blood, the trans fats are converted to triglycerides, a high level of which can increase cardiovascular problems, and raise cholesterol levels.

Smoking

Smoking increases the occurrence of free radicals, using up the body's supply of vitamin C, thereby increasing the risk of arteriosclerosis. It also introduce nicotine and carbon monoxide into the blood. Nicotine constricts the blood vessels, exacerbating the risk of thrombosis or heart attack. Carbon monoxide encourages blood clotting and reduces oxygen levels in body tissues and muscles, including the heart muscle. Regular cigarette smoking is thought to increase the risk of cardiovascular disease by at least 100 per cent. Both cigarette and cigar smokers are at risk of oral cancers, whether or not they inhale.

The body's remarkable ability to recover is underlined in the risk factors for smoking. Just ten years after stopping smoking, the likelihood of cardiovascular complications will have reduced to almost the same as that of someone who has never smoked. This means that it is always worth giving up smoking, whatever your age and no matter how long you have smoked.

Hypertension

If the flow of blood through the circulatory system is impeded, the internal circumference of the arteries is reduced. This is one of the main reasons for high blood pressure. Taking a blood pressure reading gives a clue about the condition of the intima (the internal layers of the arteries and veins). A high reading may indicate the presence of atherosclerosis.

Lack of exercise

A lack of regular exercise has been proved to have a detrimental effect on the cardiovascular system. Take regular aerobic exercise to work all muscles, including the heart muscle itself, increasing its capacity and endurance. As the heart beats harder, blood flows faster, ensuring better delivery of nutrients and oxygen to every part of the body, as well as more efficient removal of waste by the blood. Exercise also increases levels of the HDL 'good' cholesterol, which works in our favour.

Alcohol

Apart from the fact that excessive alcohol leads to weight gain and raised blood pressure, alcohol also encourages platelets in the blood to become stickier. This makes the blood thicker, impeding its passage through the blood vessels.

However, a small amount of alcohol, particularly red wine, does have some beneficial effects. Red wine contains a substance called quinone, an antioxidant that can help to reduce cholesterol and prevent plaque deposits. Two or three glasses a week are thought to be beneficial, but more than this can be harmful. Alcohol also encourages the excretion of magnesium, and this mineral is essential for a healthy heart.

Diabetes

The condition known as type 2 diabetes mellitus (see page 10) carries with it the risk of hypertension. The diabetic's body produces large quantities of insulin, yet the circulating sugar in the blood does not respond to it, so the smallest blood vessels can become coated in sugar (glycosolated). This makes the risk of heart disease up to ten times greater than for those who do not suffer from this type of diabetes.

nutrition know-how

The omega-3 essential fatty acids found in oily fish, sunflower and pumpkin seeds reduce blood coagulation. Eating a handful of these valuable seeds every day, and a portion of fish 3–4 times per week, is recommended.

Family history

It is thought that 25 per cent of the population has an increased risk of heart attacks due to

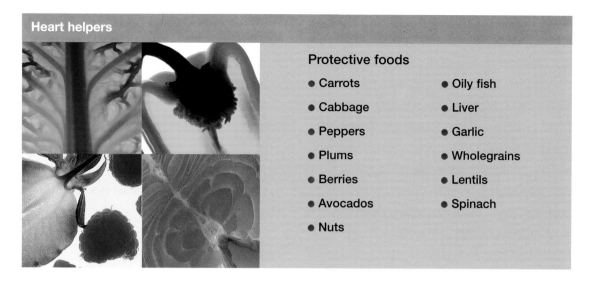

Heart helpers

Protective foods

- Carrots
- Cabbage
- Peppers
- Plums
- Berries
- Avocados
- Nuts
- Oily fish
- Liver
- Garlic
- Wholegrains
- Lentils
- Spinach

genetic disposition. This is thought to be linked to arterial deterioration which occurs in people not expected to be at high risk (they have never smoked, take regular exercise, have good diets, maintain their correct weight and have normal blood pressure). Generally, if there is a family history of heart disease, extra care needs to be taken with diet and lifestyle.

A minority of people, estimated to be roughly 1 in 500, suffers from a condition known as familial hypercholesterolaemia. This genetic error causes unusually high levels of cholesterol to circulate in the blood. Families with hypercholesterolaemia have to be particularly vigilant about their diet (making sure they avoid all saturated fats) and lifestyle choices.

Homocysteine

Recent research has confirmed the involvement of another possible genetic factor in heart disease. Homocysteine is a protein metabolite which, like all other products of metabolism, needs to be cleared from the body efficiently. In some people it can build up, to detrimental effect.

It has been found that certain vitamins, namely B6 and B12, are often deficient in those with high homocysteine levels in the blood. Taking a supplement of these vitamins, together with the amino acid methionine, can help clear pathways, preventing long-term damage.

Research has been going on in this area for over 30 years, but the medical profession has taken a long time to recognize that this genetic factor may play an even larger part in the development of heart disease than cholesterol. Tests to measure homocysteine levels are now readily available, and form part of a thorough diagnostic cardiovascular screening.

Stress

Stress is an unavoidable part of life. Continued stress encourages the body to release adrenaline, which is responsible for making the blood thicker and stickier. This is part of the 'fight or flight' syndrome (see page 55–57), when the body responds to danger or challenge. Excess adrenaline in the blood is eventually converted into a substance called adrenochrome. This has free radical properties that can lead to the first stage of atherosclerosis, because the intima (internal layers) of the arteries are damaged.

Continued stress stimulates the breakdown of bone, releasing stores of calcium into the blood. This encourages calcification of the arteries, as well as potentially increasing the risk of osteoporosis (for more on this condition, see page 59). Stress also encourages the excretion of magnesium (see page 59–60). The balance of these two essential minerals is crucial to the health of smooth muscle tissue found in the heart itself: calcium precipitates its contraction and magnesium its relaxation.

Salt

In the body, salt (sodium) and potassium are delicately balanced in all cells. Together, they are responsible for maintaining water levels in the cells, and the intake/output of nutrients and waste matter. If there is additional salt coming into the body through the diet, this balance is disturbed, resulting in increased blood pressure.

Salt occurs naturally in food. For example, raw broccoli contains approximately 0.25 per cent sodium and carrots contain approximately 0.3 per cent. While this may not sound like much, someone eating just three portions of vegetables a day is easily getting enough sodium for the body.

Eating any processed food – whether it is a snack, a ready meal, or even canned vegetables – will cause an excessive amount of sodium to be taken in by the body. Food manufacturers use a lot of salt in their products because it is cheap and provides some flavour.

If you feel that you can't taste your food and have to put salt on it, then you may be deficient in zinc. Check this for yourself by taking the zinc test on page 64.

To get the best out of your taste buds, you need adequate amounts of zinc. Talk to your nutrition consultant about taking a zinc supplement, as quantities of this mineral should not exceed 45 mg per day.

The cholesterol connection

Cholesterol used to be much feared. Less than 20 years ago it was thought to be the major cause of heart disease. Although it is certainly a contributory factor, it is important to remember that our bodies actually need and manufacture cholesterol every day for vital functions.

Cholesterol is a naturally occurring substance in the body, produced by the liver in varying quantities (but usually less than 3 grams per day). It is used in cell membranes and for the formation of hormones; it is required for the synthesis of vitamin D, and in the nervous system it is a constituent of the myelin sheath, the protective covering on all nerves. Usually, any excess cholesterol in the body binds with fibre and is excreted via the bowels. However, if large amounts accumulate, they can cause the

nutrition know-how

Grapefruits are a rich source of vitamin C and bioflavanoids, good for protecting the health of the arteries. Eating two or three per week provides ample vitamin C as well as being a good additional source of fibre to lower cholesterol.

formation of gallstones, or may be stored as fat in cellulite, or seen as small white or yellowish spots just below the eyes.

There are two types of cholesterol: high-density lipoprotein (HDL) and low-density lipoprotein (LDL). The two balance each other. The HDL removes cholesterol from vulnerable areas, taking it back to the liver for recycling and disposal, while the LDL does the opposite – it delivers cholesterol throughout the body to where it is required. Both are carried in the blood.

nutrition know-how

The perfect meal for heart health would include some fish, at least two types of vegetables and a little wholegrain brown rice. This provides high levels of protein, EPA, antioxidants, B-complex vitamins, calcium, zinc and magnesium.

The ratio between the two should ideally be 3:1 in favour of the HDL. However, many of us have raised levels of LDL and reduced HDL, upsetting the ideal balance and allowing the potentially harmful cholesterol to build up in the body.

The facts are clear – LDL cholesterol levels are increased by a high intake of saturated fats. These fats are found in red meat, full-fat dairy products and fried foods. The more of these foods that we eat, the higher our cholesterol levels are likely to be.

However, if the amount of cholesterol taken in from dietary sources is too high, a healthy body will reduce the amount it produces accordingly.

Cholesterol can also build up if there is too much in the blood, or it is not excreted because of a lack of fibre in the diet.

Heart diseases

We will now look at some of the diseases and conditions that can affect the heart and circulatory system.

Arteriosclerosis

In this condition, the arteries thicken due to calcium salts from the blood being deposited in the arteries, or because of the deterioration of the connective tissue of the heart. This thickening leads to a loss of elasticity, which in turn reduces the flexibility of the blood vessels. Although often considered to be part of the normal process of ageing, many factors can contribute to increased, and possibly unnecessary, incidence of arteriosclerosis. The condition is very common, and together with atherosclerosis (see below), it is one of the primary causes of heart attacks and strokes. Nutrition plays a powerful role in avoiding these conditions.

Atherosclerosis

The arteries are lined with a layer of smooth tissue, known as the intima, which can become coated in a plaque not unlike the one that builds up on teeth. In time, this plaque forms a lesion of irregular cells.

In an attempt to repair the lesion damage, more smooth muscle cells are produced. But the damaged cells do not divide correctly and substances constantly flowing past in the blood, such as LDL cholesterol (from trans fats), calcium and platelets attach to this mass, making it grow larger and narrowing the space available for the blood to pass through.

In time, the internal circumference of the artery is reduced as the damaged area grows. Other lesions that have broken away further along the flow can then become lodged in the narrowed artery, causing a blockage.

Depending on where the blockage actually occurs, the resulting starvation of oxygen will either cause a heart attack (if it is in the circulation around the heart) or a stroke (if it is nearer the brain).

There has been much research into how the arteries become damaged in the first place, creating the need for repair, and it is thought that free radicals play a major role. This means that there is a need for antioxidants, which protect the intima. Vitamin C in particular is required for maintaining the integrity of the arterial wall and research has shown that it can effect repair.

Angina pectoris

Angina simply means 'pain', and 'pectoris' means 'in the chest': angina pectoris is chest pain. This is a common condition.

It results from what is known as 'ischemia', which is a reduced blood flow to a part of the body. If blood flow is limited, the area suffers a reduction in oxygen and nutrient supply. This has the effect of compromising the capacity of the cells without actually destroying them. The heart has its own blood supply to keep it working. When ischemia occurs, the heart continues to pump as hard as usual, but it is not receiving enough oxygen and nutrients to support its exertions.

Angina comes on after a period of this unsupported exertion, perhaps following exercise or climbing the stairs. Symptoms include pain in the middle of the chest, arms and jaw, dizziness and weakness.

Heart attack (myocardial infarction)

A heart attack happens when the blood supply to the heart is cut off by a blockage, either in the blood vessels leading to the heart, or in the circulation within the heart muscle itself. As we know, heart attacks can be fatal. However, many people do survive them, because the severity of the attack depends on where in the heart the blockage has occurred.

If someone survives a heart attack, areas of the heart tissue will have died and are replaced by scar tissue. Scar tissue is not flexible, leading to a reduction in the heart's ability to function normally. Imagine trying to blow up a balloon where one part of it is covered in sticky tape – that part remains solid and inflexible, reducing the amount of air that the balloon can take. Apply this to the heart, and it's obvious that it will have not have the capacity to

nutrition know-how

Avocados are known as the 'perfect fruit', because they contain all the antioxidant vitamins and are particularly high in vitamin E, which is the most protective nutrient for the heart.

pump as much blood as before. There are three stages in the build-up to a heart attack. They are as follows:

Step 1 – A combination of high blood pressure and accumulated free-radical damage (which has not been balanced out by a sufficient intake of antioxidants) is thought to damage the intima. A lesion forms.

Step 2 – Plaque collects at the damaged site, and other substances in the blood attach themselves to it. The plaque grows, causing an increase in blood pressure. The body is always vigilant and aware of damage, and having sensed a problem, it will send more white blood cells to the affected area. These cells simply add to the plaque. More free radicals are produced through a series of events, causing further damage, and so the cycle starts again.

Step 3 – A piece of the plaque breaks away under the pressure of the blood rushing past, and blocks an artery. Part of the heart is deprived of its oxygen, and a heart attack occurs.

Stroke

Stroke is the third most common cause of death in the UK. It affects many people in their 40s and 50s, as well as those who are older. Simply put, a stroke is similar to a heart attack, except that the brain is the target organ. The arteries carrying oxygen and vital nutrients to the brain become impeded by atherosclerosis or arteriosclerosis (or both), causing arterial narrowing and the risk of blockage. If the brain is starved of oxygen for more than a couple of minutes, corresponding brain damage will inevitably occur. Various parts of the body's motor co-ordination will be affected, depending on which artery is involved, and which parts of the brain are damaged. For some, the effects are relatively minor, such as the inability to move a limb; whilst for others, the effects are devastating, causing total paralysis to one side of the body or, at worst, bringing immediate death. For the fortunate ones, partial or even total recovery is possible, although this can take months or even years, because the affected nerve transmission is slow to repair.

The causative factors are many – genetic susceptibility, high-fat diets, being overweight or obese, high blood pressure, raised HDL cholesterol levels, lack of exercise, a sedentary lifestyle, and the ageing process.

Nutritional approaches for avoiding stroke include a diet low in saturated fats, regular consumption of oily fish to reduce the accumulation of arterial cholesterol, and a high intake of fibre. Vitamin E is essential to reduce platelet aggregation and lower blood pressure, as well as neutralizing free-radical damage.

High blood pressure

There are several causes for high blood pressure. One of the most common today is stress, which raises circulating cortisol levels (see page 58–59

nutrition know-how

Cooking with turmeric can help reduce cholesterol levels as it contains curcuminoid, a substance shown to have a positive effect on 'bad' cholesterol. Indian cooking includes many soluble fibres and vegetables in its spicy curries, which balance the saturated fats of the chicken, lamb and beef dishes.

on stress), causing the arteries to constrict and blood pressure to rise, as in the 'fight or flight' syndrome. Whilst this is appropriate on occasion, in situations where the body needs to be on the alert, the more commonplace scenario of continual 'executive stress' is both long-term and damaging. Other contributors to high blood pressure include smoking, regular alcohol consumption, an excess of salt, high intake of animal (saturated) fats, and obesity. Stimulants

throughout the day, replace them with herbal teas, plenty of mineral water and fruit or vegetable juices. Beans and legumes contain soluble fibres that also have cholesterol-lowering properties. They are an excellent source of vegetable protein, and should be enjoyed frequently, replacing some of the meals based on animal protein. Black-eyed beans, kidney beans and barlotti beans make a delicious as well as nutritious contribution to recipes.

To keep the whole circulatory system running smoothly and efficiently, the heart must be kept in prime condition. The arteries and veins serving it must remain flexible and free of blockages, and this is where good nutrition is vital.

such as coffee, tea and alcohol are major culprits. The answer to beating high blood pressure is a change of lifestyle, rather than attempting a quick fix (like short-term measures to get you through an insurance medical). High blood pressure is one of the body's warning signs: don't ignore it. Start cutting out processed foods, smoked products and convenience foods, and increase eating lean proteins. Do not add salt to your cooking or to meals – this can upset the delicate balance of the sodium/potassium pump (see page 125–126). There is already sufficient salt present in all foods. Eat fewer dairy foods, and replace animal proteins with other sources such as fish, nuts and seeds.

Fresh vegetables and fruit provide necessary antioxidants and should form a large part of the day's meals. If you usually sip stimulant drinks

Regular exercise is essential for lowering high blood pressure, but if you have not exercised for some time, it should be undertaken with care. Seek the advice of your medical practitioner to establish the most suitable form for you.

Varicose veins

Whilst a hereditary factor is often implicated in the occurrence of varicose veins, there are other considerations to be taken into account, in which diet and lifestyle play a large part. Carrying excess weight will burden the veins in the pelvis and legs, placing extra strain on the valves that encourage the regular flow of blood back up towards the heart. In addition, the walls of the veins may become damaged because of high pressure and sluggish lymphatic drainage, which leads to the bulging blue veins associated with this condition. Jobs that involve standing up all day, such as hairdressing, tends to increase the likelihood of varicose veins, as gravity also places a burden on the valves. For the same reason, it is important to avoid crossing the legs when sitting, to ensure unimpeded blood flow.

From a nutritional perspective, it is important to include plenty of vitamin C and bioflavanoids in your meals. Vitamin C is excellent for protecting the intima layer and the walls of veins and arteries throughout the body. Bioflavanoids also strengthen the walls, preventing them from weakness and bulging. Both vitamin C and bioflavanoids are found in particularly rich supply in dark red berry fruits and citrus fruits, especially grapefruit. In the winter months, when cherries and blackcurrants are unavailable, you can substitute the tinned variety, because their nutrient content is well preserved by this method of storage.

Poor circulation

If you often get cold hands and feet, it's likely that you suffer from poor circulation, the causes of which are similar to those for varicose veins. A slow-moving lymphatic system, the over-consumption of saturated fats (such as those found in animal produce), smoking and a high salt intake can all contribute to sluggish circulation, as can lack of exercise.

Stopping smoking is essential. Increasing fibre in the diet, to remove saturated fats and cholesterol, is important. Make vegetables and legumes a main part of meals. Fruits containing vitamin C and bioflavanoids, such as strawberries, raspberries, kiwi fruit, citrus fruits, currants and berries will all help to improve the condition.

Thrombosis

A thrombosis occurs when a blood clot (thrombus) forms within an enclosed, undamaged blood vessel. Blood clotting usually occurs as a natural part of the healing process after an injury has damaged skin, organs or body tissue, in order to prevent excessive loss of blood. Blood should not clot, however, if there has been no damage.

If a clot builds up in an artery leading to the heart (this is known as a coronary thrombosis), it will prevent the essential flow of blood carrying oxygen and nutrients, and cause a heart attack. Likewise, a thrombus in the arteries leading to the brain is a common cause of stroke. A thrombus can form anywhere in the body, such as in the legs, intestines, eyes or kidneys, giving rise to extreme pain and loss of function. If a fragment of a thrombus breaks off (called an embolus), the results can be equally damaging, as it may cause a blockage in another part of the body (an embolism).

The causes of both thrombosis and embolism are the same as for atherosclerosis. In each case, the delicate balance of blood clotting mechanisms has been disrupted by smoking, a high intake of saturated fats, excessive amounts of sugar and sweetened foods, obesity and lack of exercise. Dietary factors are extremely important in regaining health – the reduction of red meats, sugars, processed and fast foods will allow the arterial damage to repair itself. Vitamin C is vital for arterial repair, as is vitamin E, which is the most important antioxidant for neutralizing damage to the intima of the blood vessels by cholesterol and saturated fats.

Essentials for a healthy heart

Maintaining the health of your heart is crucial if you want to lead a long, healthy and happy life. If you look after your heart, you will be able to maintain fitness levels and keep busy and active into old age. So, take note of the following factors.

- Make sure your diet is low in saturated fats. Avoid foods high in sugars or refined carbohydrates.

- Take regular exercise, such as walking, swimming and cycling.

- Eat foods rich in vitamin C, vitamin E, beta-carotene, essential fatty acids, zinc and selenium.

- Do not smoke.

- Do not drink more than the recommended amount of alcohol. (7–10 units of alcohol a week for men and women should be the maximum.)

Essential fatty acids from the omega-3 group are vital for balancing the blood clotting mechanisms throughout the circulatory system.

Most people in the West tend to have a higher intake of omega-6 essential fatty acids, because of the foods commonly eaten. This imbalance can be redressed in favour of the omega-3 group by increasing the amount of oily fish in the diet, such as salmon, tuna, herring, mackerel and sardines. Regular consumption of flaxseeds (linseeds), pumpkin and sunflower seeds has the same beneficial effect.

Blood clotting

The phenomenon of blood clotting is a familiar one – when we suffer a cut, the blood that oozes out of the wound soon thickens and forms a clot, stopping the escape of the precious fluid. This forms the initial stage of repair to the injured site. Two components of the blood are responsible for clotting. The blood platelets work in conjunction with a protein called fibrin. The platelets coagulate into a mass that the fibrin can fasten on to. Fibrin is converted from fibrinogen. It is possible for a doctor to measure fibrinogen levels: a high level indicates that the patient is at risk from heart disease.

In heart disease, platelets can clump together in the bloodstream. Studies have shown that people who have just had a heart attack, or who are at high risk of one, have higher levels of platelet aggregation in the blood.

Heart nutrition

Having now examined some of the factors involved in cardiovascular disease, it should be clear why certain nutrients and foods are recommended for a healthy heart. The Fighting Five – vitamins A, C, E and the minerals selenium and zinc – are essential heart nutrients.

such as antacids and analgesics (pain killers), the liver will not be able to emulsify and break down the dietary fats, causing a build-up of cholesterol and other lipids.

Regular consumption of diary goods, animal meats and rich foods slow down the digestion,

Regular aerobic exercise is important for clearing excess cholesterol as well as working the heart muscle. Include walking, swimming or cycling in your weekly repertoire to invigorate the circulation.

The antioxidant properties of these five nutrients help to quash the free radicals that are produced as a natural by-product of metabolism (see page 124) – oxidative damage, as we have seen, plays a major part in arterial damage. Even more free radicals are produced as a result of smoking, pollution and eating fried foods.

The importance of digestion

A healthy digestive system is vital to absorb the nutrients required for optimum heart function.

'Heartburn', or indigestion, is often an early indication of the type of daily stress the heart has to cope with. Insufficient hydrochloric acid in the stomach will not allow proteins to be broken down, causing a burning sensation and an 'over-full' feeling. This can occur after an evening meal, when going to bed soon after eating paces extra strain on the digestive system.

If the liver is already overleaded by frequent drinking, over-the-counter or prescription drugs

which results in constipation and toxins being re-absorbed into the bloodstream.

In order to improve digestion generally and benefit from the following heart nutrients, observe the following guidelines:

- Eat small meals regularly throughout the day.
- Chew your food well to aid proper digestion.
- Ensure that at least five to seven portions of fruits and vegetables are consumed every day to increase the fibre content, removing excess cholesterol from the digestive tract.
- Drink only small amounts of fluids at meal times to prevent the digestive enzymes from being diluted.
- Eat plenty of foods that help liver function. These include asparagus, artichokes and beetroots.
- Include raw vegetables juices regularly in your diet, as they contain high levels of nutrients.
- Eat a light evening meal.

On the next few pages we look at each antioxidant individually, as well as discussing some other beneficial nutrients for the heart.

● Vitamin A

Vitamin A comes in two forms, and it is beta-carotene that is most important as an antioxidant. Beta-carotene also strengthens blood capillaries.

Good sources: red, yellow and orange fruits and vegetables such as peaches, peppers, plums and berries.

● Vitamin C

Vitamin C is perhaps one of the most powerful nutrients for combating cardiovascular disease. It has been shown to lower cholesterol levels by reducing LDL and increasing HDL. It helps regulate blood pressure by thinning the blood and has powerful antioxidant properties.

Good sources: strawberries, kiwi fruit, potatoes and oranges.

● Vitamin E

Vitamin E has many benefits for the cardiovascular system. It strengthens blood vessels, reduces blood viscosity (stickiness), regulates the heartbeat and increases levels of HDL while at the same time protecting LDL from harmful free radicals.

Many nutrients work more efficiently in conjunction with another. Vitamin E is understood to work especially well with selenium to protect the cardiovascular system.

Warning: Take care with vitamin E if you are on heart medication (such as an anti-coagulant, for example Warfarin). If you are taking this type of drug, always check with your doctor before taking vitamin E supplements. (In such cases, high doses – 800 iµ daily – are not recommended. Your doctor may advise you to take small doses at first, building up to 400 iµ a day over three months.)

Good sources: wheatgerm oil, oily fish such as salmon and mackerel, nut oils, eggs, green vegetables and avocados.

● Selenium

The body makes antioxidant compounds and enzymes to combat naturally occurring free radicals. One of these antioxidant enzymes is called glutathione peroxidase, and the body requires selenium for its production. Selenium is a mineral found in the soil.

Modern farming pressures require farmers to grow crops year after year in the same fields, which greatly depletes the selenium content of the land. Vegetables grown in soil that is rich in the mineral will have a higher selenium content than those grown in a more impoverished soil. Even eggs have a variable selenium content: if chickens eat feed that iis high in selenium, their eggs will contain a high level of it.

Good sources: liver, fish, seafood, sesame seeds, wholegrains, onions and garlic.

● Zinc

Zinc is required for the synthesis of the natural antioxidant super oxide dismutase (SOD). To test your own levels of this important nutrient, turn to the test on page 64.

Good sources: shellfish, wholegrains such as rye and buckwheat, almonds and cashews.

● **Magnesium**

The balance of potassium and sodium in the body affects blood pressure, and this balance is regulated by magnesium. For this reason, magnesium deficiency can cause an increase in blood pressure.

Magnesium works with calcium in all muscles and is responsible for their ability to relax. As the heart muscle contracts and relaxes more than any other in the body, a lack of magnesium can affect the rhythmic action of the heart and lead to arrhythmia (irregular heartbeat). Surgeons often prescribe magnesium supplements after heart bypass operations.

If you eat a lot of refined sugars and alcohol, it encourages the excretion of magnesium, so cut down on these.

Good sources: fish, seafood, lentils, soya, beans, nuts, seeds, dried fruits and green leafy vegetables.

● **Co-enzyme Q10**

This remarkable nutrient is involved in energy production at a cellular level. Each cell has a tiny power plant in it – the mitochondria – which burns fuel to make energy. The more physical exertion we undertake, the greater the number of mitochondria we have, because they multiply according to the body's requirements. As the hardest working muscle in the body, the heart has one of the highest numbers of mitochondria. Therefore, ensuring high levels of co-enzyme Q10 assists the heart muscle in its constant work. It is interesting to note that co-enzyme Q10 can be made in the body from

other enzymes, but our ability to do this declines as we age. We can also get co-enzyme Q-10 directly from the food that we eat. In Japan it is common to take supplements, and this is becoming more widespread in the West.

Good sources: sardines, mackerel, green beans and spinach.

● **B vitamins**

The B group of vitamins are all essential for energy production. However, vitamins B3, B5 and B6 are extra-important for preventing cardiovascular disease.

● **B3**

Vitamin B3 comes in two forms: niacin and niacinamide. Niacin can cause a flushing sensation because it dilates blood vessels. It is for precisely this reason that it is so useful in protecting the cardiovascular system – dilating blood vessels helps keep blood pressure down.

Both types of vitamin B3 reduce LDL and raise HDL, as well as being effective in the treatment of diabetes, a condition which carries with it a high risk of cardiovascular disease (see page 107).

Good sources: green leafy vegetables, such as kale, spinach and cabbage and wholegrains including millet and rye.

● **B5**

Vitamin B5, or pantothenic acid, can increase HDL levels, improving the ratio between the good and bad cholesterols. It is also involved in reducing stress.

Good sources: firm, green vegetables, such as brocolli and brussels sprouts, as well as barley and wholegrain brown rice.

....

● B6

Vitamin B6, or pyroxidine, together with vitamin B12, is essential for preventing the build-up of homocysteine, which can be partly responsible for the 'furring up' of the arteries.

Good sources: whole grains, liver, kidneys, eggs and vegetables including cabbage, watercress and parsley.

....

● Oils and fats

One type of oil, known as eicosapentaeoic acid (EPA) has been shown to lower blood pressure, reduce LDL and raise HDL and lessen the adhesion of platelets, and therefore the stickiness of the blood.

As EPA is an oil, it has double bonds in its chemical structure and these double bonds are vulnerable to free radicals. Always balance oils and fats with anti-oxidants.

Another type of fat, known as saturated fat, should be avoided because it can encourage raised LDL and blood triglycerides, and also contribute to the 'clogging' of arteries that is involved in conditions such as arteriosclerosis and atherosclerosis.

Good sources: nuts and seeds, fish (especially cold water fish such as mackerel, salmon, haddock and sardines). Health authorities suggest that we should all eat oily fish at least three times a week, but we suggest that you try to eat it five times a week and also have a handful of nuts every day.

....

● **F**ibre is essential for maintaining healthy heart function, as it is required for the removal of excess cholesterol from the digestive tract. Inadequate fibre allows the re-absorption back into the circulatory system from the gut.

There are two types of fibre – soluble and insoluble. Soluble fibre is found in the soft pulp of fruits such as strawberries, peaches nectarines and plums. Insoluble fibre is found in wholegrains and pulses (legumes) such as wild and brown rice, sweetcorn, black-eyed beans, kidney beans and lentils. Include at least two to three sources of either type of fibre every day.

Good heart snacks

It is more beneficial for the heart if you eat meals regularly, rather than the more traditional three meals a day. This is especially true of a heavy dinner which exerts additional pressure on the heart to supply the rest of the body with the nutrients it needs. Good snacks include:

- Stewed apples and blackberries
- Grapefruit and orange-segment fruit salad
- Avocado dip on rye cakes
- Tahini (sesame seed dip) on oatcakes
- Sardines on ryvita
- Salmon on buckwheat blinis
- Spinach salad with pine nuts
- Tuna and sweetcorn salad
- Lentil and carrot soup
- MIxed vegetable and barley soup

cancer

Cancer is a blanket term for a group of over 100 different conditions. Some names are all too familiar, such as breast or lung cancer. These are very common diseases; other cancers, such as pancreatic cancer, are less well known because they have a lower incidence.

It is widely recognized that diet and lifestyle play an important role in the formation and spread of cancer. In this chapter we will examine how best to protect ourselves against cancer.

We all have cancerous cells within us, because they occur naturally. It is the job of the immune system (see page 83) to clear them away. However, the creation of an environment conducive to the proliferation of these cells into what we know as cancer, is largely up to us. We can influence our chances of getting the disease enormously through diet and lifestyle.

It is important to understand that nutrition consultants cannot, by law, 'treat' cancer. But we are often called in by a patient or his doctor to provide essential nutritional support. If a patient is being treated with conventional methods, then we can tailor a nutritional programme to reduce the side-effects. Some patients refuse chemotherapy, preferring more natural methods, in which case we can assist in creating a programme that will support their immune systems as fully as possible.

How does cancer start?

Healthy cells replace themselves when they are damaged or worn out. This process of replication and replacement is usually carried out on a regular basis in a carefully controlled manner. Sometimes cells continue to replicate, but without control or order. The excess cells form new, independent tissue with their own blood supply, and this is the basis of a tumour. Many of these areas of new tissue are benign (posing no threat) and can be removed by surgery or left alone.

Some tumours are malignant. These are damaging because they contain cancerous cells that grow unchecked and can spread to other parts of the body to form more tumours.

Normal cells can become cancerous through exposure to carcinogens, or through genetic predisposition. The genes that are thought to have the ability to alter the characteristics of a cell are known as oncogenes. Oncogenes develop from normal genes called proto-oncogenes, which are involved in the day-to-day

LEFT Broccoli is part of the anti-cancer, cruciferous family of vegetables.

functioning of cells. Many factors can contribute to encouraging a proto-oncogene to become an oncogene, amongst them changes in DNA (see below), which is thought to mutate after contact with a carcinogen or virus. Oncogenes produce huge amounts of factors that stimulate the growth of mutated cells.

The growth of cancerous cells occurs for three main reasons: DNA damage, immune system problems, and injury to cell membranes.

DNA

Our genetic code is contained within a chemical called DNA. Each person's unique DNA make-up provides a blueprint for the manufacture of cells in the body. For example, if new cells are required in the digestive tract, the body knows what sort to create because it is programmed into the DNA.

However, if the DNA is damaged in any way, perhaps by free radicals, toxic chemicals or viruses, the formation of new cells can be adversely affected. To understand this, imagine a photocopier. If the original document fed into the machine has a blemish on it, the copies that are replicated will have the same blemish. If the machine is incorrectly programmed, it may produce 50 copies rather than the one copy you required. In a similar fashion, DNA sometimes produces too many damaged or immature cells. The extra cells then form a tumour.

Immune system problems

The immune system is responsible for clearing away cell debris, in addition to cells that have not formed properly. You can read more about this in the section on the immune system (page 81–89). If the system is overworked, or not well supported by adequate nutrition, it becomes vulnerable. Mutant cells are not attacked and disposed of, allowing them to proliferate.

Cell membranes

Through various mechanisms, the outer membrane layer of the cell can become damaged, leading to rapid cell division.

Cancer triggers

Most of us have heard stories about people who have smoked 60 cigarettes a day for 70 years and never had a day of illness in their lives. It would seem that there are triggers that will set off the cancer process. These people obviously didn't have a trigger that responded to cigarette smoke

Common carcinogens

● Smoking	● Burnt food	● Fried food
● Nitrates	● Nitrites	● Ultraviolet light
● Alcohol	● Radon gas	● Pesticides
● Asbestos	● Chlorine	● Fluoride

– nicotine and tobacco were not carcinogens for them. Perhaps their trigger was alcohol, and had they indulged in alcohol regularly, the outcome might have been different.

Some people may have more than one trigger, so cancer could result from any number of carcinogens, such as smoking, drinking alcohol and eating barbecued/burnt food, combined with a compromised immune system. Again, this underlines our biochemical individuality.

Categories of cancer

There are many types of cancer, which fall into four main categories.

● **Leukaemias** are cancers of the tissue involved in the formation of blood, such as bone marrow. In this case, abnormal blood cells replicate out of control.

● **Carcinomas** are cancers that affect the layer of tissue that lines the external and internal surfaces of the body – the epithelium. The areas most at risk are glands, organs, skin and mucous membranes. The epithelial cells mutate, and are then produced too rapidly, and are often malformed in some way.

● **Sarcomas** are cancers that form in connective tissue and so can appear in any part of the body such as fat, muscle, blood or lymph.

● **Lymphomas** are cancers of the lymphatic system (see page 105–106), which contains lymph – the fluid that 'bathes' body tissue. Lymph is filtered through the lymph nodes, whose role is to protect against infection and trap carcinogens, which makes them vulnerable to cancer.

How does cancer grow?	
Initiation	The cells and tissue appear normal, yet minute changes are taking place within the cells. These changes initiate the process of cancer.
Promotion	The tissue alters as the new cells replicate out of control, forming a tumour. If, for any reason, the tissue were to be examined, the changes would be visible.
Progression	The cancer increases in size as more new cells are synthesized. The tumour now requires nutrients and oxygen of its own, so it creates a blood supply. This is done at the expense of the surrounding tissue.
Malignancy	The cancer has now taken hold and is unlikely to respond to any diet or lifestyle changes. Surgery, chemotherapy and radiology may be required to remove it.
Metastasis	The cancer migrates or travels to other parts of the body, leading to secondary tumours.

Free radicals, antioxidants and cancer

Free radicals are molecules that damage the body's DNA and cell membranes. They are closely linked to the initiation and spread of cancer. They are produced in the body as a normal by-product of metabolism. Sunlight, smoking, and fried foods all create free radicals.

To disarm these potentially damaging free radicals, the body needs antioxidants. Imagine an apple cut into two halves, with lemon juice poured over one half and the other left as it is. After a few minutes, the untouched half will start to react with the oxygen in the air and turn

The body also manufactures its own antioxidants, such as two antioxidant enzymes produced in the liver, superoxide dismutase (SOD) and glutathione peroxidase (GP). These both rely on nutrients for their formation. SOD is found in two forms: one requires manganese and iron, the other zinc and copper. GP requires selenium for its construction. All these minerals are found in fresh nuts and seeds, dark green leafy vegetables and wholegrain products. Including such foods in your meals every day should ensure that your body is supplied with the nutrients it needs to produce enough vital natural antioxidants.

'Prevention is better than cure' and we cannot ignore the importance of fresh food as part of a healthy lifestyle. Raw food will always offer a greater level of all the nutrients, so get as much as you can, even if only in the form of fruit and juiced vegetables.

brown. The half covered in lemon juice will retain its original colour. The lemon juice has exerted a protective effect, acting as an antioxidant. The same sort of thing happens in the body, where antioxidants protect against damage by free radicals.

Anti-cancer foods

The first step in protecting yourself against cancer is to reduce your exposure to things that promote free radicals: give up smoking, cover up in the sun, and avoid fried foods. However, you can also help your body to maintain an adequate level of antioxidants, for example by eating foods containing antioxidant nutrients.

Nutrition and cancer management

For those who already have cancer, good nutrition can play a powerful role in its management. There are three main nutritional aims: to support the immune system, to assist in detoxifying and protecting the body from the effects of the cancer and medical treatment, and to enhance the effects of conventional medicine, where possible.

Cancer cells thrive in oxygen-free environments. Good nutrition helps to defeat them by ensuring that all body tissues are well oxygenated. Cancer cells also flourish on arachadonic acid, which is one of the products of the metabolism of fats.

Some arachadonic acid is essential but too much can encourage inflammation, in addition to creating a pro-cancerous environment. Excess arachadonic acid can often be avoided by removing saturated fats from the diet, such as full-fat milk, hard cheese and red meats. Eating lots of fresh fruit and vegetables, as well as fresh nuts, seeds and wholegrains, assists the successful conversion of fats into anti-inflammatory fats.

Cancer cells are also thought to thrive in the sugar-rich environment created by a diet that is high in refined sugars and alcohol.

It is important to note one thing. We are not saying that a diet high in fats and sugars *will* lead to cancer, but that the risk will be increased if these foods are chosen instead of fresh foods that are thought to offer protection.

Cancer treatment and nutrition

Treatments for cancer include surgery, hormone therapy, immunotherapy (boosting the body's own immune system with drugs), radiotherapy and chemotherapy. All these treatments tax the body, so having a first-class nutritional support regime is essential.

For example, during chemotherapy, chemicals are administered to attack the cancer cells. However, they also damage the surrounding healthy cells. Common side-effects range from hair loss and a drop in weight, to confusion, depression and lethargy. This therapy is very demanding on the body. We feel that it is imperative to support the immune system with optimum nutrition at this time.

It is important to understand some of the dietary principles that reduce the production of free radicals, and the environmental conditions that the development of cancers favour.

All body tissue has different levels of acidity and alkalinity but, overall, it functions best in a mildly alkaline state. Prolonged acidity within the body is pro-cancerous, and the typical Western diet (fried foods, food additives, colourings, sugar, salt, chemically treated food, excessive amounts of animal protein and dairy products) creates over-acidity.

High acidity can be combated by following an oriental macrobiotic diet, which is highly alkaline. This means an abundant vegetable intake, low consumption of fats (avoiding all animal and dairy produce, which is high in saturated fats) and a regular intake of foods with properties known to reduce the development of cancers such as soya beans, soya products and sea vegetables – seaweed, dulse, and carrageen.

Cell function is regulated by a delicate balance of the minerals sodium and potassium. There is a greater amount of potassium inside each cell and a greater amount of sodium outside it. Together they

nutrition know-how

Use fresh miso (a paste made from soya beans) as a stock base for risottos, soups and sauces. It provides potent anti-cancer properties without any of the chemicals often found in stock cubes and powders. Add one teaspoonful to boiling water.

create an electrical charge, not unlike that of a battery inside a torch. This is known as the sodium/potassium pump and it regulates which nutrients can enter the cell and which waste matter can leave it.

The Western diet is unhealthily high in salt, which is added to virtually every prepared foodstuff, primarily for 'taste' but also for its preservative action. This greatly disturbs the sodium/potassium pump, allowing for an increased possibility of cancer development. Max Gerson, who developed the Gerson method of naturopathic cancer treatment, advocated a high-potassium diet, similar to the diet our cavemen forefathers would have eaten. Potassium is found in abundance in raw, unprocessed plant foods, including all vegetables and fruits. Choose organic produce, which is free from chemicals, pesticides and fertilizers.

Balancing blood sugar levels is a vital part of cancer prevention. There is an increase in glucose metabolism with the onset of cancer, and this stimulates greater production of insulin. Once a cancer has started to develop, it will feed directly on blood glucose. Most importantly, the immune system is compromised by elevated levels of circulating blood glucose.

Saturated fats (found in animal produce) have a direct bearing on the development of cancer. Our cell membranes must remain fluid for the intake of nutrients and the clearing of toxic waste, in the same way as the sodium/potassium pump mentioned above. The most important nutrient for preventing the development of cancer is oxygen, as cancer cells cannot survive

in the presence of it. But if you eat a lot of saturated fats, it causes the cell membranes to become rigid, inhibiting their uptake of oxygen. Abnormal cell development can then continue unchecked.

nutrition know-how

Help your liver to clear excess oestrogens by including plenty of B vitamins, especially B2 in your diet. Excess oestrogen may increase the risk of hormone-based cancers in women such as cancer of the breast and the ovaries. Almonds are particularly rich in B2 and make a quick and tasty snack.

Fibre is essential for digestive health – and for the prevention of colon and rectal cancers. Many studies have looked at the influence of diet on different types of cancer, investigating both immediate and long-term effects. Fibre in the colon creates a more acidic environment, which is less friendly to carcinogens.

Nitrites and nitrates are used to cure ham, beef, hot-dogs, bacon, sausages, fish and cooked meats. These contain similar carcinogenic compounds to those found in tobacco smoke. These types of food, in addition to barbecued and/or burnt foods, should be limited. Tasty though they are, the damage caused by regular consumption is simply not worth it. The antioxidant vitamins A and E are especially important for neutralizing these damaging chemicals in the stomach, where nitrosamines are produced from nitrites and nitrates.

Alcohol has recently been found to be one of the most carcinogenic substances that we consume. Combined with smoking, its effects are increased many times over. While the occasional drink is acceptable, regular intake interferes with the process of detoxification by the liver and exposes the mouth, throat and oesophagus to potentially harmful chemicals. The picture is rather more serious for women than men because, if liver detoxification is reduced or impeded, excess oestrogens cannot be cleared efficiently and this may exacerbate the risk of the hormone-related cancers of the breast, ovaries and uterus.

Anti-cancer foods

There are many foods that are now recognized to have potent anti-cancer properties. The saying that 'prevention is better than cure' could not be more applicable. With current estimations foretelling an incidence of the disease of almost one in two by the year 2005, we simply cannot ignore the importance of fresh food as part of a healthy lifestyle. Raw food will always offer a greater level of all the essential nutrients, so get as much as you can, if only in the form of fruit and juiced vegetables.

We are already familiar with the Fighting Five group of antioxidants which help the immune system function efficiently. These vitamins and minerals all play a vital role in preventing cancer cells from getting out of control. However, there are also other foods that have anti-cancer properties, and it is well worth including them in our daily diet.

The cruciferous family

This group of foods includes broccoli, cauliflower, cabbage, brussels sprouts, bok choy and watercress: all renowned as potent anti-cancer weapons. They contain indoles, which stimulate the production of the antioxidant enzyme glutathione peroxidase. It is believed that indoles inactivate excess oestrogens, which can cause cancer, particularly of the breast. These vegetables also contain good levels of vitamin C, a potent antioxidant, and should be eaten raw wherever possible to preserve their indole content, or lightly steamed.

Soya beans and soya products

Soya beans and any products made from them such as tofu, tempeh, miso and soy sauce, prevent abnormal cell growth. They also contain isoflavones and phytoestrogens, both of which have anti-cancer properties. A further benefit is that these foods have been found to reduce the toxic side-effects of chemotherapy and radiation.

Garlic and onions

Garlic acts as a chelator, which means that it latches on to and carries away toxins from the body, including potentially cancerous heavy metals such as cadmium from cigarettes. Onions behave in the same way as garlic, although to a lesser degree. They both contain allicin, a sulphur compound which is a potent detoxifier. In addition, garlic stimulates the white blood cells that consume cancer cells.

One of the commonest forms of cancer is stomach cancer, but a regular intake of both garlic and onions can reduce the likelihood of developing this disease. Garlic is also a rich source of sulphur, required by the liver for effective detoxification. As the liver is the clearing-house for all potentially cancer-forming chemicals and pathogens passing though the body, the importance of this humble vegetable cannot be underestimated.

Kelp

Kelp contains a rich source of iodine, which is essential for the health of the thyroid, the gland that regulates blood sugar (energy) metabolism. It is a well-known fact that the thyroid starts to shrink from the mid-twenties onwards and many people are found to have hypothyroidism (insufficient production of thyroid hormones) at this time.

If energy production is lowered, the body's blood sugar metabolism alters to adapt, which can be pro-cancerous. Kelp contains abundant amounts of selenium, which is a potent antioxidant. (See the Fighting Five, page 116.)

Almonds

These nuts contain leatrile, a natural compound that contains a cyanide-like substance deadly to cancer cells. The ancient Greeks, Romans, Egyptians and Chinese all consumed seeds and stones from fruits such as apricots, as they believed them to have anti-cancer properties. Conventionally, leatrile has been used as an anti-cancer treatment, but not as a food source.

Oriental mushrooms

Maitake, shiitake and rei-shi mushrooms contain powerful, immune-stimulating polysaccharides known as beta-glucans. These are not found in ordinary mushrooms, so it is worth seeking out these Eastern gems, even in dried form, from supermarkets and Chinese food shops. Use them in any recipe that calls for mushrooms.

Tomatoes

These fruits have received much recognition in the last few years for their anti-cancer properties. They are rich in lycopene, a powerful antioxidant which is believed to be more effective than vitamin A and beta-carotene.

Carrots

Like most orange-coloured vegetables, carrots are one of the richest sources of beta-carotene (the precursor to vitamin A), one of the Fighting Five antioxidants. Interestingly, the craze for consuming large amounts of juiced carrots as a cancer therapy, especially to treat breast cancer, misses an important point: a large amount of essential nutrients are lost in the juicing process, not to mention fibre. It is necessary to eat plenty of raw carrots as well as juicing them.

Citrus fruits

Citrus fruits and cranberries contain bioflavonoids: these support and boost the antioxidant quality of vitamin C, which these fruits have in rich supply.

Peppers

These contain capsaicin, which is believed to block the cancer-forming compounds found in smoked and cured meats and fish. Peppers are also an excellent source of beta-carotene, particularly red peppers.

Seeds

Linseeds, pumpkin seeds, sunflower seeds and sesame seeds all cotnain lignans, compounds that are found in the tough outer husk of the seed. Lignans are phyto-oestrogens (that is, they actually mimic the hormone oestrogen) and may help reduce excess oestrogens circulating in the body – the excess oestrogens are known to stimulate hormone-based cancers, such as breast cancer, ovarian cancer and uterine caner.

Eating one tablespoon per day of these mixed seeds is thought to be beneficial. Mix the seeds with 'smoothies' (see the recipes on pages 130–155), and try them in fruit salads, and in fruit juices on cereals (granolas). You can also add them to salads, soups and stews. Soya beans, tofu, miso and tempeh are all good sources of lignans, which could be one of the reasons why the Asian countries have a lower incidence of hormone-related cancers.

Raw Power

The benefits of raw food in cancer prevention is vital. Ideally, at least 50 per cent of daily intake should be raw. Juiced fruit and vegetables are excellent, as they contain a condensed level of all the antioxidant nutrients, but these should be complimented by raw salads, vegetable cruditeés and fruits to help eliminate toxins from the digestive tract.

Beta-carotene foods

The carotenoid family of fruits and vegetables are rich in beta-carotene, an essential part of the antioxidant team.

The richest sources of these are oranges, lemons, cantaloupe melons, mangoes, papaya, tomatoes, red, yellow and green bell peppers, carrots, kale, broccoli, spring greens, spinach, collards, squash, sweet potatoes, apricots and peaches.

Recipes

All recipes cater for 4 persons, including the tofu smoothies for breakfast. All measurements are in metric as well as imperial. However, only follow one set of measurements. If at all possible, try to buy organic versions of all the ingredients listed in the recipes.

Recipes for a Healthy Digestive System

Raw and fresh fruits and vegetables alll contain digestive enzymes, which reduce the digestive load on the body. Raw juices are particularly beneficial. Onions, garlic and rice are all known to have a calming effect on the digestive system as a whole and, even in the most severe cases of digestive disruption, any of these three foods can have a settling effect. The fibre found in fruit, vegetables and wholegrains is important for maintaining proper bowel function, and preventing constipation.

BANAPPLE TOFU SMOOTHIE

Bananas and apples contain pectin, which helps remove toxins and excess cholesterol from the digestive tract. It also encourages the growth of beneficial bacteria in the gut, which is essential to maintain harmony and prevent the overgrowth of bad bacteria such as *Candida albicans*.

Many digestive complaints are of an inflammatory nature, so pumpkin seeds are an important part of this drink as they contain plenty of the omega-3 essential fatty acids, which have an anti-inflammatory effect throughout the body. You could also use sunflower or sesame seeds.

Grind the seeds in a coffee grinder if your food processor is not strong enough, as they can irritate an inflamed digestive system if eaten whole.

Ingredients
3 teaspoons of pumpkin seeds
400 gm (14 oz) of organic tofu, drained and cubed
2 bananas
2 medium unpeeled apples, quartered and cored
1.5 litres (3 pints) of rice milk or oat milk

Method
Grind the seeds in a food processor or coffee grinder to release their essential fats and prevent any irritation in the gut. Add the remainder of the ingredients and blend for 1–2 minutes until smooth.

PEPPER-PARSNIP SOUP

Parsnips are known to improve bowel function and to detoxify and cleanse the digestive tract. Because they tend to taste quite sweet, this soup is suited to those who enjoy creamy, mild soups rather than a more complex taste. Peppers contain good antioxidants for reducing the damage caused by bacterial infection, as well as being an excellent intestinal cleaner.

Ingredients
5 tablespoons of olive oil
1 medium onion, peeled and chopped roughly
560 gm (20 oz) of parsnips, peeled and cut into chunks
2 red peppers, washed, cored and de-seeded
1.1 litres (2 pints) of vegetable stock
½ teaspoon of ground nutmeg

Method
Heat the oil in a heavy-based saucepan over medium heat, then sweat the onions for 2 minutes. Add parsnips and cook for a further 5 minutes, stirring occasionally. Add chopped peppers and stir for 1 minute, then pour in the stock and add nutmeg. Simmer for 15–20 minutes until parsnips are softened and then transfer to blender. Blend until smooth, then reheat and serve.

REAL ONION SOUP

Onions are one of the most soothing vegetables for the digestive system. Onions alleviate the pain associated with stomach and duodenal ulcers, and steaming them brings out their natural sweetness. They are naturally anti-spasmodic, antiseptic and antibacterial and so should be eaten daily if you suffer from digestive problems. The active component in the onion is allicin, an anti-inflammatory compound which is most potent when eaten raw. However, this soup (without the traditional cheese added that would make it too rich for those with digestive upsets) keeps cooking time to a minimum to preserve this valuable ingredient.

To make the soup more substantial, you can add 250 gm (9 oz) of rice noodles, which should be stirred into the soup after the flour has been mixed in.

Ingredients
450 gm (16 oz) of onions, peeled, halved and sliced lengthways 'with the grain'
3 tablespoons of olive oil
1.1 litres (2 pints) of vegetable stock
2 teaspoons of soy sauce or tamari
25 gm (1 oz) of plain or rice flour

Method
Heat the oil gently in a heavy-based saucepan and add all the onions. Cover with a lid and sweat the onions for 10 minutes, stirring once or twice to prevent sticking or browning. The onions should be transparent, not burnt. Add stock and soy sauce or tamari. Stir and cook for a further 15–20 minutes over a low heat. Mix the flour in a ladle-full of the soup.

Blend, then return to the saucepan and mix in. Stir until soup thickens slightly (approximately 5 minutes more) and then serve.

ROASTED BEETS

Beetroots are excellent for detoxifying the liver. They are also a good intestinal cleanser for the excesses of the holiday seasons or after eating too much rich foods. Raw beetroot juice is the most nutritious way of consuming these wonderful little vegetables, but many people find the taste too earthy and strong. However, we have found that roasting them slowly brings out their natural sweetness, without destroying all their nutrients.

These are delicious hot as an accompaniment to a chicken or game dish, or eaten cold as an appetizer when sliced over a green salad and dressed with an oil and balsamic dressing.

Ingredients
4 medium beetroots
1 tablespoon of olive oil
1 teaspoon of low-sodium sea salt

Method
Wash the beetroots (but do not skin) and cut back the shoots and roots to within 1.5 cm (½ in) of the beetroots itself. Rub each beetroot with a little olive oil and place on a baking sheet. Sprinkle with sea salt and then place in a moderate oven 175ºC (350ºF) for 45–60 minutes, depending on size. When cooked, they should be firm, but will give a little when pressed with an implement.

CHICKEN CHUNGA

A chunga is a Caribbean word for a hotpot, into which virtually anything can be thrown. Traditionally, most chungas are fish based. However, chicken has always been known for its calming effect on the digestion because it helps to break up the excessive mucus in the digestive tract. It is a high source of protein, which is excellent for convalescence. The vegetables included in this chunga are only a suggestion – experiment to see which combination works best for you. Serve with brown rice.

Ingredients

1 medium chicken, quartered (giblets removed)
Juice of 2 lemons
1 large onion, peeled and chopped
2 medium carrots, scrubbed and sliced
100 gm (4 oz) of button mushrooms
1 medium red pepper, cored, de-seeded and chopped
125 gm (4½ oz) of black-eyed beans, soaked overnight
1 stick celery, chopped
3 tablespoons of olive oil
1 tablespoon of fresh ginger, peeled and chopped
1 small red chilli, de-seeded and chopped finely (optional)
1 tablespoon of rice flour
1 glass of white wine
300 ml (10 fl oz) of chicken stock

Method

Remove the skin and any fat from the chicken pieces. Place them in a bowl of water with the juice of 2 lemons. Leave for 1 hour. Meanwhile, prepare all the vegetables. Simmer the black-eyed beans in water for 45–50 minutes until just beginning to tenderize. Drain and set aside. Heat the olive oil in large casserole dish, and sweat onions until transparent. Add the ginger and chilli, if using, and the carrots, celery and red pepper. Stir until you start to smell the aromas. Remove all the vegetables from the casserole and put to one side. Take the chicken out of the lemon water and pat dry with kitchen towel. Lightly sauté the chicken pieces in the ginger and chilli oil until sealed, then remove and put aside. Sprinkle the rice flour into the oil, a little at a time, and mix thoroughly. Add the white wine and stir until it starts to thicken and the alcohol is burnt off. Pour in the chicken stock and simmer for 5 minutes to allow it to thicken further before putting in the chicken and vegetables. Finally, add the mushrooms, stir again, and place in a medium oven at 180ºC (375ºF) for 1½ hours.

LEMON SOLE WITH SESAME OIL

Lemon sole is a delicious, light fish that is easily digested and can be bought throughout the year. Buy a whole fish and ask your fishmonger to fillet it for you as the fish is likely to be fresher this way. Poaching fish is the best way to retains its nutritional benefits, as it can be cooked at a low temperature. Sesame seeds contain important anti-inflammatory essential fatty acids, but they can be irritating to the digestive tract if it is not in a healthy state. By using the oil, you can benefit from these essential fats without risking any discomfort.

Ingredients

2 teaspoons of Dijon mustard
2 teaspoons of tomato purée
60 ml (2 fl oz) of milk
Ground black pepper

4 lemon sole fillets
1 tablespoon of olive oil
4 tablespoons of sesame oil
1 teaspoon of rice flour

Method

Mix together the Dijon mustard, tomato purée and milk. Season with ground black pepper. Place the lemon sole fillets in an ovenproof baking dish, and pour over the milk sauce. Cover with foil and place in oven at 175°C (350°F) for 25–30 minutes, until the fish is cooked through. Remove the fish, place on a heated plate and cover. Pour the milk mixture from the baking dish into a small saucepan and place over a gentle heat. Mix the sesame oil and rice flour into a paste and whisk into the sauce until it thickens.

Pour over the lemon sole fillets and serve.

AVOCADO AND ARTICHOKE SALSA

Avocados are rich in vitamin E which has great soothing and healing qualities for digestive problems. They are rich in vitamins and minerals and have a high protein content, making them a perfect base for a lunch-time snack. Combined with artichoke hearts, which stimulate the beneficial bacteria in the gut, and olive oil, this salsa is a gentle yet potent dish. You can serve this dish with raw vegetable crudités or oatcakes.

Ingredients

2 large ripe avocados
6 medium artichoke hearts in olive oil (fresh or bottled)
2 teaspoons of soy sauce or tamari
Juice of 2 lemons
Ground black pepper

Method

Halve the avocados, discard the stones and scoop out the flesh. Cut the artichoke hearts into quarters, reserving a few leaves for garnish. Place the avocados, artichoke hearts, olive oil, soy sauce and lemon juice in the food processor and blend thoroughly, stopping just before the dip becomes completely smooth. Season with ground black pepper to taste.

COTTAGE CHEESE AND MILLET SALAD WITH PINEAPPLE AND ORANGE

This is an easy-to-prepare lunch or supper dish which is full of vital nutrients. Cottage cheese is an excellent form of low-fat protein, while pineapple contains bromelain, an inherent digestive enzyme, which will lift the burden from an overworked digestive system. Millet is a good source of fibre for regulating bowel function and is also low in allergenic properties. It is also very alkaline, which suits the intestinal environment and is good for the beneficial bacteria that should reside there. Lastly, the oranges are full of vitamin C, an important antioxidant.

Ingredients

8 tablespoons of olive oil
250 gm (9 oz) of millet grain
750 ml (26 fl oz) of vegetable stock
2 tablespoons of lemon juice
100 gm (4 oz) of cottage cheese

2 celery stalks, trimmed and finely sliced
2 fresh pineapples, cut into chunks
1 orange, peeled, and cut into segments
2 tablespoons of chives

Method

Gently heat 2 tablespoons of olive oil in a heavy-based saucepan and add millet grain. Stir until grain begins to 'pop'. Add the vegetable stock and simmer for 20 minutes. Drain the millet, spread it out on a baking dish and leave to cool. Meanwhile, whisk the remaining olive oil and lemon juice together to form a vinaigrette and stir into the cooled millet. Allow to stand for 10 minutes for the flavours to be absorbed. Add the cottage cheese, celery, pineapple, orange segments and chives to the millet and mix well. Chill before serving.

SWEET POTATO CRUMBLE WITH RYE

Sweet potatoes are highly nutritious and easily digested. They contain excellent levels of vitamins C, E and beta-carotene which are all antioxidants essential for 'mopping up' the toxins produced by faulty digestion and bacterial infections. They are renowned for calming inflammations of the digestive tract and ulcers.

This recipe is actually delicious cold and could be served as a lunch-time dish with some natural yoghurt for added protein, or with a simple side salad for a light meal.

Ingredients

3 large sweet potatoes, peeled and
   roughly chopped
1 bay leaf
2 tablespoons of olive oil

Black pepper to taste
2 teaspoons of grated nutmeg
200 gm (7 oz) of fresh rye breadcrumbs
1 tablespoon of finely chopped parsley

Method

Simmer the sweet potatoes in water with the bay leaf until they are just becoming tender. Drain, return to pan and add half the olive oil and black pepper. Add the nutmeg and combine in a blender or food processor, or mash until smooth. Place the mix into a ceramic baking dish. Gently heat the remaining oil in a heavy-based pan and lightly brown the breadcrumbs. Add the chopped parsley and mix thoroughly. Place the breadcrumbs on top of the sweet potatoes and bake in moderate oven at 180ºC (350ºF) for for 30–40 minutes or until golden.

CHERRY FLUFF

Cherries are naturally anti-spasmodic and can be very soothing for those with an irritable bowel complaint. The bioflavanoids and vitamin C they contain encourage healing of the collagen in the intestinal walls. You can use either fresh or canned cherries as, unlike many other fruits, the nutrient content is not lost in the canning process. Organic, live bio-yoghurt contains acidophillus which is one of the main beneficial bacteria found throughout the intestinal tract. This pudding takes only a couple of minutes to make and is suitable both for a children's tea party and a formal dinner.

Ingredients   **450 gm (16 oz) of cherries, fresh or tinned (unsweetened)**
500 gm (18 oz) of organic, live natural bio-yoghurt
Several sprigs of fresh mint to garnish

Method   Remove the stalks and stones from the cherries. Combine with the yoghurt and one sprig of mint in a blender or food processor and blend until smooth. Chill for 1 hour before serving. Serve in individual ramekins or dessert glasses and garnish with sprigs of mint .

GINGER AND MINT TEA

Ginger contains anti-spasmodic qualities and helps to quell nausea. It is also used to relieve morning sickness during pregnancy. This gentle, calming tea will sooth your stomach when digestive upsets prevent you from eating anything at all, as well as relieving cramps and indigestion caused by fatty foods. Peppermint is used in hospitals for its potent calming elements which reduce gas and associated discomfort after abdominal surgery. Make a large batch and store the remainder in the fridge for up to 2 days.

Ingredients   **450 gm (16 oz) of fresh root ginger, peeled and thinly sliced**
6 sprigs of fresh peppermint, washed
1.1 litres (2 pints) of still mineral water, boiled.

Method   Place the sliced ginger and mint into large heat-proof jug and add the hot mineral water. Leave to stand for at least 15 minutes before drinking.

Recipes to help the immune system

Stimulants such as tea, coffee and alcohol, recreational and prescription drugs, as well as pollution, all induce the production of free radicals. A strong immune system will combat disease on a daily basis, providing it is well supported. Foods rich in antioxidant nutrients – vitamins A, C, E, and the minerals zinc and selenium – are found in fresh fruits, vegetables, fish, wholegrains, and nuts and seeds.

RUBY TOFU SMOOTHIE

We recommend these smoothies to nearly all our clients, as they are filling and provide a good ratio of protein to carbohydrates and fats. Strawberries are one of the richest sources of vitamin C, as are blackcurrants and raspberries. They also contain bioflavanoids which work with vitamin C to support the immune system. However, the potency of vitamin C diminishes with exposure to light, heat and air, so drink the smoothie within half an hour of making it. The sunflower and pumpkin seeds contain the essential fatty acids required for optimal cell membrane integrity, allowing beneficial nutrients to flow in, and toxins flow out of the cells. They have an important contribution to optimum immune function.

Ingredients
3 tablespoons of sunflower seeds
1½ tablespoons of pumpkin seeds
500 gm (18 oz) of either strawberries, raspberries or blackcurrants, or any combination of the three, preferably fresh
400 gm (14 oz) of organic tofu, drained and diced
1½ litres (3 pints) of rice milk or oat milk

Method
Place the sunflower and pumpkin seeds in food processor and grind for 30 seconds. Add the tofu, strawberries, raspberries, blackcurrants and rice or oat milk. Blend until smooth and serve immediately.

WARM APPLE MILLET PORRIDGE

Organic millet is rich in the minerals zinc, selenium and manganese, all of which are required for a healthy immune system. Soaking it overnight will help its natural enzymes to activate the digestive process in your body, making it easier to break down and absorb, as well as providing an excellent source of fibre.

Ingredients
250 gm (9 oz) organic jumbo millet flakes
500 ml (18 fl oz) unsweetened apple juice
100 ml (4 fl oz) rice or oat milk

Method
Soak the millet flakes overnight in the unsweetened apple juice. The next morning, gently heat in a heavy-based saucepan for 8–10 minutes, adding the rice or oat milk if more a liquid consistency is required.

MIXED VEGETABLE CHOWDER

Soups are an excellent standby and can be eaten as a snack, appetizer, or as a meal in themselves. We advocate regular soup-making as it is quick, easy and highly nutritious. The vegetables used here are all high in the antioxidant nutrients, beta-carotene and vitamin C, and the corn contains plenty of zinc, one of the Fighting Five potent antioxidant minerals.

Ingredients

2 teaspoons of extra virgin olive oil
1 tablespoon of butter
2 onions, peeled and chopped
1 stick of celery, washed and chopped
175 gm (6 oz) of carrots, peeled and sliced
225 gm (8 oz) of winter squash or
  butternut squash, chopped
175 gm (6 oz) of potatoes, peeled and diced
2 tomatoes, skinned and chopped.

175 gm (6 oz) of broccoli florets, stalks
  trimmed
100 gm (4 oz) of corn (either canned or
  stripped from the cob)
1 litre (1¾ pints) of vegetable stock
125 ml (4½ fl oz) of low fat yoghurt,
Unsweetened or soya milk
Handful of basil leaves, torn, not chopped.

Method

Heat the oil and butter gently in heavy-based saucepan and then add the onions. Cook for approximately 5 minutes until transparent. Add the celery, carrots, squash and potatoes. Stir for five minutes, stirring frequently to prevent browning. Add the vegetable stock, cover the pan and simmer gently for 10 minutes until the vegetables are beginning to soften. Add the broccoli, corn and tomatoes and cook for a further 5 minutes. Remove from the heat. Allow to cool slightly, then put the contents into a blender or food processor. Blend coarsely (for less than 1 minute) to thicken the soup, but without losing the colours. Add the torn basil leaves and serve with toasted rye bread or Arizona corn bread (see page 147).

SAUTEED CABBAGE WITH FENNEL

Cabbage stimulates the immune system as it has generous amounts of vitamins C and E, both of which are good antioxidant nutrients. It also has strong antiviral, antibacterial and anti-mucus properties, which makes it ideal for colds and flu, either steamed or juiced raw. Here it is combined with fennel seeds, which are also rich in vitamin C.

Ingredients

1 tablespoon of extra virgin olive oil
2 cloves of garlic, peeled and crushed
2 shallots, peeled and finely sliced

1 tablespoon of fennel seeds
275 gm (9½ oz) of shredded Savoy
  cabbage or other dark green cabbage

Method

In a large, heavy-based frying pan, gently heat the olive oil for a minute and then add the garlic, shallots and fennel seeds. Cook for a further 2–3 minutes until the garlic and shallots soften. Add the cabbage and stir-fry continuously for another 2 minutes until just softened.

Serve as an accompaniment to fish, chicken or game dishes.

CLASSIC TABBOULEH WITH SEAWEED

Bulgar wheat (also known as cracked wheat) contains a rich source of minerals, including zinc and selenium which are both potent antioxidant nutrients. Tabbouleh has a clean, refreshing taste and the tomatoes, cucumber and onions all contain vitamin C for protection against infection. However, the addition of the seaweed gives it a completely different flavour and increases the levels of selenium for added immune system fortification.

This is an excellent accompaniment to a fish dish or serve it on its own for a lighter meal. This dish should be eaten as fresh as possible, so try not to make it too far in advance as the flavours will mingle, even if refrigerated.

Ingredients

225 gm (8 oz) of bulgar wheat

4 small spring (green) onions, trimmed, and chopped finely

1 medium cucumber, washed and diced with skin left on

2 firm tomatoes, washed and with seeds removed, diced and peeled.

1 large green bell pepper, washed, de-seeded and finely diced

50 gm (2oz) of parsley, finely chopped

25 gm (1 oz) of dried flaked Kombu (seaweed) available from large supermarkets

or 50 gm (2oz) of finely chopped fresh seaweed from the fish counter

I bunch of fresh mint, finely chopped

3 tablespoons of olive oil

3 tablespoons of fresh lemon juice

½ teaspoon of ground cumin

Ground black pepper for seasoning

Method

Soak the bulgar wheat in 600 ml (1 pint) of cold water for 30 minutes, then drain and squeeze out excess moisture. Set aside. Soak the dried flaked Kombu seaweed (if you are using it) in bowl of warm water until rehydrated. Toss the bulgar wheat with the parsley, mint and Kombu or other seaweed and then add all the vegetables. Mix the olive oil, lemon juice and cumin together. Grind in some black pepper to taste and mix thoroughly into the salad. Add a little more lemon juice if required for taste.

SUNRISE PEPPER SALAD

The peppers in this colourful salad contain high levels of vitamin C and beta-carotene, as well as selenium from the sesame seeds, all of which are important immune boosters and potent anti-oxidants. This salad makes an excellent light lunch that can easily be prepared in advance.

Ingredients

1 medium yellow pepper

1 medium red pepper

1 medium orange pepper

2 teaspoons of sesame seeds

3 tablespoons of extra virgin olive oil

1½ tablespoons balsamic vinegar

Several fresh basil leaves

Method
Wash all the peppers and rub with about a third of the olive oil. Place into a baking dish and cook in the oven at 180°C (350°F) for 30–35 minutes or until the skins have begun to shrink but not blacken. Remove from oven and place the peppers in a plastic bag for 25 minutes. This makes the skins easier to remove. Once skinned, cut in half lengthways, remove the cores and seeds and slice thinly, lengthways. Mix the olive oil, balsamic vinegar and a little ground black pepper in a small dish. Pour over the peppers and toss thoroughly. Place on a serving dish and sprinkle with the sesame seeds. Garnish with a few fresh basil leaves.

POACHED PRAWNS (SHRIMPS) IN GINGER BROTH WITH RICE NOODLES

Prawns (shrimps) are a rich source of zinc and selenium, which support the immune system. Zinc is also essential for healing and rebuilding body tissue. Carrots contain abundant supplies of beta-carotene (vitamin A) which, as an antioxidant, is an important Fighting Five nutrient for combating free radicals.

Ingredients
750 ml (26 fl oz) of vegetable stock
2 teaspoons of fresh, sliced ginger
1 red onion, peeled and finely sliced
1 medium leek, washed, trimmed and finely sliced
1 large carrot, scrubbed, and finely sliced

1 teaspoon of chilli oil
800 gm (28 oz) of fresh, peeled pink prawns
50 gm (2 oz) of dried rice noodles
3 teaspoons of soy sauce
Fresh coriander leaves to garnish

Method
Gently heat the stock and soy sauce in a heavy-based saucepan and add the ginger, onion, leek and carrot. Simmer for 10 minutes. In another saucepan, lightly sauté the prawns in chilli oil for 1 minute. Add them to the vegetable stock, together with the rice noodles. Simmer for three minutes and then serve in deep, warmed soup bowls. Garnish with coriander.

ACORN SQUASH RISOTTO

Risottos are easy to make, and will make a nutritious, tasty side dish or a complete meal. Acorn (or butternut) squash contains a rich source of beta-carotene and vitamin C for boosting the immune system, while rice is packed with B-vitamins for energy production. Onions are also known to be naturally antiviral and antibacterial.

Ingredients
1 tablespoon of olive oil
25 gm (1 oz) of unsalted butter
100 gm (4 oz) of onions, peeled and finely chopped
400 gm (14 oz) of Arborio risotto rice or wholegrain brown rice
250 ml (9 fl oz) of vegetable stock

120 ml (4¼ fl oz) of dry white wine
250 gm (9 oz) of acorn squash, peeled, de-seeded and coarsely chopped

Method
2–3

Heat the butter and oil in a heavy-based frying pan. Sauté the chopped onion for approximately minutes, until transparent. Add the rice and stir until it is coated with the butter, onion and oil mixture – or until you hear the rice start to 'click'. Meanwhile, heat the vegetable stock in another pan and add a ladle of it to the rice, stirring continuously to ensure that the rice does not stick to the bottom of the pan. Pour in the wine and allow the rice to absorb it fully, before continuing to add the vegetable stock, a ladle at a time, until it is all absorbed (reserve one ladle to be added after the acorn squash).When thick and creamy, and the rice still *al dente*, stir the squash into the risotto, allowing it to cook and break down slightly. This should take approximately 4–5 minutes. Turn off the heat, add the last ladle of stock and stir in. Allow to stand for 2–3 minutes and then serve in warm, flat soup or pasta bowls. Add a little fresh parmesan cheese and plenty of ground black pepper.

....

AUBERGINE, TOMATO AND ROSEMARY BAKE

Aubergines (eggplants) are a good source of beta-carotene, and tomatoes contain lycopene, another of the carotenoids (as beta-carotene) which has been found to be a potent immune-system booster. Aubergines (eggplants) have a tendency to absorb a lot of olive oil, which can make this dish rather rich if the first steps outlined in the recipe are not followed.

This dish is perfect as a light meal or as an accompaniment to fish or poultry. You could also melt a small amount of feta cheese over it.

Ingredients
1 medium aubergine (eggplants), trimmed
   and sliced
1½ tablespoons of extra virgin olive oil
2 medium ripe tomatoes, sliced
Ground black pepper
2 tablespoons of chopped fresh basil

Method

Lightly steam the aubergine slices for 4–5 minutes in a steamer. Remove and place onto a baking sheet to which half the olive oil has been placed. Brush the aubergine slices with a little more of the oil, then put a slice of tomato on top of each piece of aubergine. Top with freshly ground black pepper and chopped basil. Bake under the grill at a medium heat for 5–6 minutes or until the tomatoes have softened.

....

Main Meals

SPINACH TORTILLA

Spinach has long been known to be a nutrient-dense vegetable, and includes both beta-carotene and vitamin C. It is important to choose very fresh spinach, as these vital vitamins will diminish rapidly with age. The potatoes in this recipe are another rich source of vitamin C, as well as immune supporting minerals (see pages 85–86). The addition of the eggs provides protein and so makes this a perfectly balanced lunch-time meal. It can also be made in advance and kept in the fridge until required.

Ingredients

450 gm (16 oz) of fresh leaf spinach
340 gm (12 oz) of potatoes, diced
1 medium onion, peeled and
    finely chopped

1 tablespoon of olive oil
425 ml (15 fl oz) of puréed tomatoes
6 medium eggs

Method

Steam the spinach in a little water until soft. Boil the potatoes for 6–8 minutes until softened, but still firm. Drain and set aside. Sauté the onion in the olive oil until transparent, then add half the puréed tomatoes and simmer gently for 3–4 minutes. Beat the eggs and divide in half. Mix one half with the spinach and the other with the potatoes. Place the spinach mixture into a heated omelette pan and cook over a moderate heat for 2–3 minutes until the mixture comes away from the pan. Place the pan under a hot grill and allow the top of the omelette to rise slightly. Remove from the grill and transfer omelette to a serving plate. Repeat with the potato and egg mixture. Spread half of the tomato mixture over the spinach omelette and cover with the potato omelette, as if making a sandwich. Finally, cover the top with the remaining tomato mixture and serve.

PEACH GRANITA

A granita is effectively a sorbet without any added sugar. Most fruits contain ample sugars of their own, so it is not really necessary to add any more. Sugar directly depletes the function of part of the immune system for up to five hours after consumption, so reducing it from your diet will automatically give your immune system – and your health – an instant boost. Peaches are rich in vitamin C and beta-carotene, as well as being a good source of fibre.

Ingredients

4 large ripe peaches, skinned, halved,
    stoned and sliced
2 tablespoons of lemon or lime juice
200 ml (7 fl oz) of water

3 star anise
1 stick of cinnamon
A few fresh strawberries or raspberries
    to garnish

Method

Heat the water in a pan until it is almost boiling and then turn off the heat. Soak the star anise and the stick of cinnamon in the water for 1 hour to infuse the flavours, then remove and discard the star anise and cinnamon. Blend the peach slices in a food processor with 2 tablespoons of the water until smooth. Add the lime juice and blend again. Place the mixture in a plastic ice-cream container and freeze until hard (4–5 hours). Take out of the freezer and serve with a few fresh strawberries or raspberries.

Recipes for Inflammation

The omega-3 group of essential fatty acids found in nuts, seeds and oily fish all contain potent anti-inflammatory compounds. Various fruits and vegetables from the nightshade family, however, including tomatoes, potatoes, aubergines (eggplant), zucchini and tobacco, have the opposite effect, contributing to the pain and inflammation associated with such conditions as rheumatoid arthritis. Free radicals are an inevitable by-product of inflammation and may be reduced by including plenty of antioxidant-rich foods such as those found in red, yellow and orange fruits and vegetables, nuts and seeds and wholegrains.

Breakfast suggestion

TOFU AND COCONUT SMOOTHIE

If you were stranded on a desert island for a week and had nothing else to eat, you could survive on coconuts alone! The vitamin, mineral and essential fat content is excellent and the coconut milk is a rich source of magnesium, potassium, zinc and vitamin C. The anti-inflammatory essential fatty acids found in this wonderful fruit are abundant, provided it is not heated.

Ingredients
400 gm (14 oz) of organic tofu
1.8 litres (3 pints) of rice milk or oat milk
240 gm (8½ oz) unsweetened creamed coconut

Method
Simply blend all the ingredients together in a blender. Alternatively, use slightly less rice or oat milk to make a thicker shake and spoon into dessert glasses with a sprinkling of nutmeg on top for a delicious pudding.

Lunch ideas

SALMON, AVOCADO AND ORANGE SALAD

Marinating raw fish in citrus fruit has the effect of 'cooking' the fish – the chemical reaction that takes place over a few hours alters the texture. This is a superb dish for anyone who dislikes the idea of raw fish, but needs the benefits that can be gained from eating it. Salmon is rich in the anti-inflammatory omega-3 essential fatty acids, which can be diminished through overheating. The juice from the oranges contains vitamin C which prevents these essential fats from oxidizing and becoming damaged. Avocados are a rich source of vitamins C, E and beta-carotene, all of which protect our body from the potential damage of inflammation in the intestines, muscles and joints.

Ingredients
500 gm (18 oz) of fresh salmon fillets
Juice of 4 limes
2 large oranges, peeled and segmented
4 small spring (green) onions
150 gm (5¼ oz) of rocket, watercress or
    baby spinach
2 medium ripe avocados, peeled,
    de-stoned and quartered

For the dressing
Marinading juice from salmon fillets
4 tablespoons of extra virgin olive oil
Grated zest from oranges
1 garlic clove, crushed
1 teaspoon of Dijon mustard
Ground black pepper

Method   Place the salmon fillets in a shallow dish and pour the lime juice over them. Cover and place in the fridge for 6 hours or overnight. Grate the zest of the orange skins and set aside for the dressing. Remove all pith from the oranges, segment them and then cut each segment in half. Wash the salad leaves and drain.

To make dressing, combine the marinating juice from the fish, which will have turned a creamy-white colour, with the olive oil, orange zest, garlic and mustard in a lidded jam jar. Shake well until all ingredients are completely blended. Add ground black pepper to taste.

Arrange the salad leaves on a plate with the salmon fillets, avocado and orange segments placed on top, and pour the dressing over the top.

TUNA IN LIME & GINGER SAUCE

Tuna fish is one of the best sources of omega-3 anti-inflammatory essential fatty acids and provides ample selenium, zinc and other minerals to support healing and repair. Ginger is one of the best root vegetables for conditioning body tissue and has anti-inflammatory and calming properties throughout the body, as it reduces histamine production. Very often, inflammatory conditions affect the body as a whole, so including ginger in many of your dishes is strongly recommended. Although spicy, this main course dish will not upset your digestive system, as the turmeric contains curcuminoids, which are anti-inflammatory compounds.

Serve with fresh, lightly steamed green vegetables.

Ingredients   85 gm (3oz) of fresh coriander
3 tablespoons of fresh ginger, peeled
  and sliced
2 cloves of garlic

3 tablespoons of lime juice
1 tablespoon of olive oil
2 teaspoons of turmeric
4 medium tuna steaks (175 gm [6oz] each)

Method   Combine the coriander, ginger and garlic in a food processor to make a paste, adding water if necessary. Mix together the lime juice, olive oil and turmeric and stir it thoroughly into the paste. Place the tuna steaks in an ovenproof dish and coat with the paste. Cover and bake in an oven for 15–20 minutes at 180°C (375°F) or until the tuna is just cooked through.

Lunch ideas

SARDINE PATE

This easy-to-make pâté is rich in oils that will help to reduce inflammation, as well as being full of protein to provide energy throughout the day. All oily fish also contain abundant vitamin E, which is one of the healing nutrients for body tissue that has been damaged by inflammation.

Serve as a delicious snack with oat or rye crackers or divide into 4 and place in the centre of a salad of mixed green leaves for a light lunch.

Ingredients
- 1 small red onion, finely chopped
- 120 gm (4¼ oz) of canned sardines in olive oil
- 1 clove of garlic, peeled and crushed
- 1 tablespoon of white wine vinegar
- 1 tablespoon of finely chopped parsley
- Lemon juice to taste
- Ground black pepper

Method
Combine all the ingredients in a food processor until blended, but not smooth. Add a squeeze of lemon juice if needed and freshly ground black pepper to taste.

TAHINI COATED CHICKEN BREASTS

Tahini is made from ground sesame seeds, olive oil, and sometimes with added garlic, and can be found in most supermarkets and health food stores. Its rich omega-3 essential fatty acid content is important for reducing inflammation. However, its oils can go rancid if exposed to light, air and heat, so it is important to refrigerate the jar of tahini once opened.

Serve with Thai white rice or organic brown rice.

Ingredients
- 4 chicken breasts, preferably organic, with skins removed
- Juice of 2 lemons
- 4 tablespoons of organic tahini
- 8 large spinach leaves
- 300 ml (10 fl oz) of chicken or vegetable stock

Method
Rub the chicken breasts in lemon juice (this is an Asian trick to kill off any bacteria that the chicken may be carrying), and cover each one with the tahini. Wrap each breast with 2 spinach leaves, overlapping them to fully enclose the tahini dressing. Secure in place with one or two cocktail sticks. Place carefully in an ovenproof baking dish and pour over the chicken or vegetable stock. Cover tightly, and cook in the oven at 180°C (375°F) for 35–40 minutes. Remove and place on a serving dish. Whisk the sauce in the baking dish to mix in any tahini that may have escaped, and pour over the chicken before serving.

WATERCRESS, WALNUT AND ALFALFA SALAD

Alfalfa sprouts are a rich source of protein and are considered to be a perfect food as they are packed with calcium, magnesium and vitamins A and E. They are also known to have excellent anti-inflammatory properties, but should not be eaten by those with auto-immune conditions such as Lupus. Walnuts are packed with essential fatty acids and vitamin E, which are important for healing, and watercress is rich in the antioxidant vitamin C, ideal for repairing damaged tissue.

Ingredients

2 bunches of watercress, washed thoroughly
100 gm (4 oz) of whole walnuts, shelled
1 tablespoon of walnut oil

2 teaspoons of balsamic vinegar
1 teaspoon of white wine vinegar
25 gm (1 oz) of alfalfa, washed

Method

Separate the watercress stems and cut off any old stalks. Shell the walnuts and discard any kernels that are shrivelled. Combine the walnut oil and the vinegars in a lidded jam jar and shake vigorously to blend the flavours. Pour over the watercress and alfalfa. Toss lightly and serve, sprinkling several walnuts over each plate.

PAPAYA, PINEAPPLE AND CRANBERRY FRUIT SALAD

Fruits are mostly alkaline, which means that they are beneficial for any kind of inflammation that tends to raise the acid level of the body. Pineapple contains bromelain, which blocks the pro-inflammatory prostaglandins, and papaya helps to reduce gastrointestinal inflammation, as well as containing plenty of the antioxidant, beta-carotene. Cranberries are probably the most alkaline of all fruits and so help to reduce inflammation in the kidneys and bladder. This rainbow-coloured fruit salad is beautiful to look at, but try not to add the cranberries until just before serving to prevent their juice from running into the others.

Ingredients

1 orange
225 gm (8 oz) cranberries, washed
1 medium pineapple
2 medium ripe but firm papaya, halved,

peeled and de-seeded
Juice of 1 lemon
225 gm (8 oz) organic, live natural bio-yoghurt or soya yoghurt

Method

Cut the orange in half, and squeeze out the juice. Put the orange juice together with the cranberries in a small saucepan and simmer gently for 15–20 minutes until softened. Meanwhile, cut off the top of the pineapple and set aside. As you will be using the pineapple to serve this pudding in, carefully scoop out the pineapple flesh, without damaging the skin, and chop into chunks, discarding the hard centre core. Chop the papaya into chunks of the same size as the pineapple and mix carefully. When the cranberries have cooled, mix with the other fruits and gently fold in the yoghurt. Pile into the pineapple shell and serve.

Recipes for the heart and circulation

Dark-red fruits and berries contain proanthocyanadins – compounds that are known to support the structure of the minute capillaries and larger blood vessels throughout the body. Oily fish contain the omega-3 group of essential fats that are thought to reduce the build-up of cholesterol plaques in the arteries and maintain general healthy heart function, while wholegrains provide the fibre needed to remove excess cholesterol from the digestive tract.

PURPLE TOFU SMOOTHIE

This smoothie provides a good ratio of protein to carbohydrates and fats. Any left-overs from breakfast can be kept in the fridge and drunk during the day. Blueberries are abundant in flavanoids, known for their artery- and blood-cleansing properties, while bananas are a rich source of potassium and magnesium, both of which are important for regular heart function. Sunflower seeds contain essential fatty acids to protect the artery membranes, reduce accumulating cholesterol and are a good source of fibre. Tofu has phyto-oestrogenic properties that regulate any excess circulating oestrogens, which may play a part in the build-up of arterial plaque.

Ingredients

2 medium bananas

200 gm (7oz) of fresh or tinned blueberries

400 gm (14 oz) of tofu, drained and diced

1½ litres (3 pints) rice or oat milk

3 tablespoons of sunflower seeds

Method

Blend all the ingredients in a blender until smooth and then serve in tall glasses. If you want to store any for later, cover tightly to prevent the air from turning the bananas brown and refrigerate.

ARIZONA CORN BREAD

This is an unrisen loaf, with the consistency of a firm cake, rather than that of a commercially produced loaf. Corn is an excellent source of fibre, essential for removing cholesterol from the digestive tract, as well as being a delicious alternative to wheat. It is rich in iron for red blood-cell health and also in magnesium for regular heart function. As this bread contains no preservatives, it should be stored in an air-tight container in the fridge.

This is delicious for breakfast with a little organic natural yoghurt poured over the top, or with scrambled or poached egg.

Ingredients

2 eggs
500 ml (18 fl oz) of rice or oat milk
2 teaspoons of baking soda

225 gm (8 oz) of yellow cornmeal
120 gm (4¼ oz) of strong brown wheat flour
75 gm (3 oz) of sunflower oil

Method

Heat oven to 190ºC (375ºF) and grease a 20 x 20 x 5cm (8 x 8 x 2in) baking tin. In a medium-sized bowl, beat the eggs until frothy. Stir in the rice or oat milk and add baking soda. Beat in the cornmeal and brown bread flour until a smooth batter is formed, with small air bubbles throughout (this is best done by hand). Pour the mixture into the baking tin and place in the centre of the oven for 25–30 minutes, or until a knife inserted into the middle comes out clean. Turn out of the tin and either serve hot or allow to cool.

CHICKPEA, PEPPER AND PINE NUT SALAD WITH CREAMY BASIL DRESSING

Chickpeas are an excellent fibre source for helping to lower cholesterol and are also rich in calcium and magnesium which help regulate blood pressure. Red peppers are an abundant source of beta-carotene, which helps protect against free radical damage to the arteries, and the vegetable protein in this dish provides ample amounts of essential amino acids to help manage blood sugar levels and provide energy.

Ingredients

300 gm (10 oz) cooked (or canned) chickpeas
1 red pepper, cored and cut into
    julienne strips
1 tomato, seeded, juiced and chopped
2 spring (green) onions, cut into julienne
    strips
2 tablespoons of buttermilk, rice milk or
    oat milk

1 tablespoon of lemon juice and pulp of lemon
1 tablespoon of white wine vinegar
1 tablespoon of olive oil
1 clove of garlic, peeled and finely chopped
1 tablespoon of pine nuts
2 tablespoons of fresh basil leaves
Several large red lettuce or radiccio
    leaves for serving

Method

In a medium-sized bowl, combine the chickpeas, pepper, tomato and spring onions. Pour the buttermilk (or rice or oat milk), together with the lemon juice, lemon pulp, vinegar, oil and garlic, into a food processor and blend until thickened. Add the basil leaves and blend again. Pour this dressing over the chickpea mixture and toss well to combine. Spoon the mixture onto the lettuce leaves and sprinkle with pine nuts. This dish will make an excellent appetizer or light lunch.

BUCKWHEAT PANCAKES

Buckwheat is not actually wheat as it comes from the rhubarb family, rather than the wheat-grain family. It is known for its cholesterol-lowering properties and is also a rich source of many minerals, including calcium and magnesium, both of which are required for a healthy circulation and heart function.

These pancakes can be made in advance and stored, with a slice of greaseproof paper or paper towel in between each pancake to prevent them sticking to each other. Store in the fridge until needed. They can also be served hot as a pudding after a main meal.

Ingredients

125 gm (4½ oz) of buckwheat flour
125 gm (4½ oz) of wholewheat flour
2 teaspoons of baking powder
2 eggs

275 ml (9½ fl oz) of rice or oat milk
1 tablespoon of sunflower oil
Small amount of olive oil

Method

Sieve both the flours and the baking powder into a large mixing bowl. Beat the eggs and then blend, together with the milk and the oil, in a food processor until smooth. Leave to stand for at least 30 minutes before using. Heat a small pancake pan over a medium flame and brush the surface of the pan with a small amount of olive oil.

Using a tablespoon of pancake mixture at a time, swill it around the pan to spread the mixture as thinly as possible. Allow to cook for 1 minute before flipping over and cooking the other side.

Serve with fresh fruits of your choice and some organic natural yoghurt for a perfectly balanced breakfast.

CARROT SOUP WITH SPINACH AND LENTILS

Carrots are known for their antioxidant nutrients, beta-carotene and vitamin C, needed for preventing the build-up of arterial plaque caused by free-radical damage. Spinach is also a good source of both of these nutrients, as well as iron, which helps carry oxygen in the red blood cells. Lentils add protein to this soup, making it more substantial, and they also contain cholesterol-lowering properties and abundant amounts of fibre.

Ingredients

450 gm (16 oz) of carrots, scrubbed
  and sliced
1 small parsnip, peeled and chopped
1 small onion, peeled and quartered
1 stick of celery, sliced

850 ml (30 fl oz) of vegetable stock
125 gm (4½ oz) of puy or red lentils
½ teaspoon of nutmeg
100 gm (4 oz) of fresh spinach, rinsed,
  with large stems discarded

Method

Add all the vegetables except the spinach, nutmeg, lentils and stock to a heavy-based saucepan and cook over a gentle heat for approximately 35 minutes, or until the lentils have softened. Remove from the heat and allow to cool slightly. Place the soup into a blender and blend until smooth. Add the spinach and blend again. Return the soup to the pan and heat through.

ARTICHOKE AND LEMON SALAD

Artichokes contain calcium and magnesium necessary for balanced heart function, liver cleansing and promoting bile function to help break down cholesterol. Lemons have a high level of vitamin C, particularly in the zest and pith, which helps to prevent the build-up of arterial plaque.

Ingredients

4 organic lemons, washed
6 small or 4 large artichokes with their
   stalks and outer leaves removed
2 tablespoons of white wine vinegar

150 gm (5¼ oz) of almonds, lightly toasted
Juice of 2 extra lemons
125 ml (4½ fl oz) of olive oil
2 tablespoons of fresh thyme leaves

Method

Wash the lemons and place them in a small saucepan with enough water to cover them. Cover with a lid and cook on a high heat for 30 minutes. Drain and cool. Put the artichokes in a large saucepan and cover with water and white wine vinegar. Cook them for 20–30 minutes, depending on size – when ready the leaves should come away easily. Take off the outer leaves if they are tough and trim the ends of the stalks. Cut the artichoke in half and remove the choke (hairy section) from the centre.

Place the artichoke halves in a large salad bowl. Meanwhile, cut the boiled lemons in half, scooping out and discarding the pulp. Cut the soft lemon skins into segments and add to the artichokes. Sprinkle over with almonds and dress with olive oil, lemon juice and thyme.

FISHERMAN'S STEW

The fish used in this recipe are high in essential fatty acids required to maintain arterial health, lower the LDL 'bad' fats (see page 110) and generally improve cholesterol levels. Fish should form the main source of protein in any heart health management programme. Garlic is a potent blood cleanser, while tomatoes provide lycopene, a beneficial antioxidant.

Ingredients

900 gm (32 oz) of fresh cod, haddock,
   halibut or salmon fillets
1 tablespoon of olive oil
200 gm (7 oz) of onion, chopped
1 clove of garlic, peeled and crushed
900 gm (32 oz) of tomatoes, washed,
   simmered, peeled and puréed (or
   900 gm [32 oz] canned tomatoes)
850 ml (30 fl oz) water

1 teaspoon of fresh basil
1 teaspoon of fresh thyme
1 teaspoon of crushed red pepper
800 gm (28 oz) of pumpkin or winter
   squash, peeled, de-seeded and cut
   into chunks
2 fresh sweetcorn, husks and outer leaves
   removed and sliced.

Method

Cut the fish into 2.5 cm (1 in) cubes. Gently heat the olive oil in a large heavy-based casserole dish. Add the onion and garlic and stir until transparent. Add tomatoes, water, basil, thyme, red pepper, pumpkin and corn. Cover, bring to boil and then simmer for 10–15 minutes or until the pumpkin and corn are cooked. Serve with chunks of rye or corn bread.

BAKED MACKEREL WITH ORANGE AND LEMON SAUCE

Mackerel is one of the highest sources of omega-3 essential fatty acids, necessary for arterial health and for lowering cholesterol levels. It is also rich in vitamin E, a blood-thinning nutrient as well as a potent antioxidant. Inexpensive and widely available, mackerel is delicious when balanced with this citrus sauce. The lemons and oranges provide ample vitamin C for the protection of the blood vessels.

Ingredients

1 small shallot, skinned and finely chopped
Olive oil
Grated rind of ½ an orange
2 tablespoons of lemon rind
Juice of 1 lemon and 1 orange
100 ml (4 fl oz) of fish stock

1 small potato, boiled and chopped
4 fillets of fresh mackerel, each approx. 120gm (4¼ oz), with bones removed, but skin left on
1 tablespoon of chives, finely chopped
4 sprigs of lemon balm or mint leaves
50 gm (2 oz) of organic natural yoghurt

Method

Sweat the chopped shallot in the olive oil over a medium heat. Add the orange and lemon rind and juice together with the fish stock and the potato. Heat through gently for 10–15 minutes to allow the flavours to meld. Put the mackerel fillets in an ovenproof dish and add one third of the fish stock liquid. Place in the oven 190°C (375°F) and bake for 10–12 minutes. Meanwhile, place the remaining stock in a blender and combine until smooth – it should have a light, creamy consistency. Pour the liquid back into the saucepan and add the yoghurt. Heat through carefully. Remove the mackerel from the oven and place on serving dishes. Pour over sauce and then garnish with lemon balm or mint leaves. Serve with wild rice and a vegetable of your choice.

ICED MANGO MOUSSE

Mangoes are one of the richest fruit sources of beta-carotene, important in the maintenance of arterial health and for antioxidant protection. This is healthy, simple to make and delicious! You can make this in advance and store in the fridge for up to 2–3 days.

Ingredients

2 ripe mangoes, peeled and sliced with the stone removed
1 small banana, peeled
3 ice cubes made from peppermint tea
75 gm (3 oz) natural organic yoghurt

Method

Place all the ingredients in the blender and mix until completely smooth. Scoop mixture into dessert dishes, and serve with a sprig of mint. This mixture could also be used for a tofu smoothie, leaving out the peppermint tea, and replacing the yoghurt with tofu.

Desserts

Recipes to help protect against cancer

It is now accepted that food may play a part in the prevention and development of some cancers. Phytoestrogens, found in soya, seeds and other vegetables, may help regulate oestrogen dominance, one of the contributing factors in hormone-related cancers. Antioxidant nutrients, found in all red, yellow and orange fruits and vegetables, seafood, wholegrains and seeds, can quench exessive free-radical production, known to be associated with the development of many cancers. It is not claimed that foods can cure cancer, but it is thought that eating five to seven helpings of fresh fruit and vegetables daily reduces the incidence per capita of cancer.

ORANGE TOFU SMOOTHIE

We recommend these smoothies to nearly all our clients as they are very filling and provide a good ratio of protein to carbohydrates and fats – the perfect way to start your day. If you want to put some aside for later in the day, place the remainder in a container and keep it in the fridge for when you need a boost. Tofu and linseeds have potential cancer-preventing properties as they are rich in phytoestrogens, which are thought to prevent the development of certain hormonal cancers. Papaya, peaches and apricots are all rich in the primary antioxidant, beta-carotene. You can use any combination of the fruits suggested below, or just one fruit at a time, in which case you will have to increase the amounts as required. If these fruits are not available, you can used the canned variety, but these are not as beneficial as fresh fruit, and you should check that the canned fruit is sugar-free. Use the syrup in the tins as well as the fruits – you will need approximately half a can of fruit per person.

Ingredients

400 gm (14 oz) of tofu
1.5 litres (3 pints) of unsweetened
   rice milk
3 tablespoons of linseeds
4 fresh apricots or 4 dried, soaked
   overnight in apple juice

1 papaya, peeled, de-seeded and
   chopped roughly
1 mango, peeled, with the stone removed
   and chopped

Method

Put all the ingredients in a blender and combine until they are completely smooth. You can store this smoothie in a refrigerator for up to 24 hours.

BREAKFAST JUICE

The juice of raw fruits are an excellent source of antioxidant vitamins. This recipe is good for cancer prevention because of its high vitamin C content. However, as these nutrients are digested very rapidly, they can tend to disturb the body's blood sugar balance, so they should be followed by some protein, such as natural unsweetened yoghurt, eggs or a small glass of Orange Tofu Smoothie, (see page 151). They are perfect for those days when you are feeling under the weather and need something to get you going, but you don't feel hungry.

Watermelon is a very rich source of vitamin C, as are strawberries. The black seeds of the watermelon are a rich source of essential fatty acids. Using fresh fruits in season is best.

Ingredients
1.1 – 1.3 kg (2½–3 lb) of watermelon, peeled, but not de-seeded
450 gm (16 oz) strawberries, with stalks removed

Method
Place ingredients in a blender in two separate batches and blend until the black seeds of the watermelon are ground. Drink immediately – this recipe is not suitable for storage.

ORANGE ROOT SOUP

This recipe contains both carrots and pumpkins, which are both rich in beta-carotene and anti-oxidants, important in cancer prevention. The added ginger gives it a zest, as well as being an excellent detoxifier and calming to the digestive tract.

To make a more filling and substantial soup, you can add before cooking 50 gm (2 oz) of macrobiotic red rice, rich in B vitamins, zinc and selenium to give added antioxidant power.

Ingredients
2 tablespoons of olive oil
1 medium onion, peeled and chopped
1 bay leaf
2 teaspoons of soy sauce or tamari
25 gm (1 oz) of fresh root ginger, washed and grated

450 gm (16 oz) of butternut squash or pumpkin, peeled and diced
450 gm (16 oz) of carrots, peeled and chopped
1 litre (1¾ pints) of water

Method
Heat the olive oil in heavy-based saucepan. Add the onion and cook gently for 3–4 minutes until transparent. Add all other ingredients, and simmer for 30–35 minutes until vegetables are soft. Remove bay leaf and put all the other vegetables into a blender. Blend thoroughly until smooth. Add black pepper to taste.

VERY VEGETABLE SOUP

Eating raw or barely cooked food is essential for building up the immune system and allowing the body to function at its best. Raw food contains many enzymes that help with digestion, and they lessen the amount of work this system has to do, particularly when it is below par. Any stress on the digestive system is potentially pro-cancerous in the long term. Cancer cells replicate more rapidly in an acid environment. It is wise to maintain a constant level of mild alkalinity in the body to reduce this potential and all the vegetable ingredients in this soup have a high potassium content, essential for maintaining the sodium/potassium balance required for an alkaline state. It is also a wonderful way of consuming a large amount of antioxidant vegetables.

Ingredients
2 large tomatoes, chopped
2 carrots, chopped
2 sticks of celery, chopped
½ small cauliflower, chopped
½ teaspoon of black pepper

2 tablespoons of chopped parsley or coriander
1 litre (1¾ pints) of organic soya milk or vegetable stock
Olive oil or butter
2 small onions, chopped finely

Method
Put all the vegetables except the onions in a blender with the soya milk and blend until completely smooth. You may have to do this in two batches, depending on the size of your blender. Heat the oil or butter gently in a heavy-based saucepan and cook the onions over a low heat until soft and transparent. Add them to the blended vegetables and simmer for 10 minutes to heat thoroughly.

ASPARAGUS AND SPINACH SALAD WITH LIME DRESSING

Asparagus contains beta-carotene and vitamin C, and spinach is part of the brassica family, which contains cancer-preventing nutrients. Sunflower seeds are rich in omega-3 and omega-6 essential fatty acids, needed to maintain cell integrity and proper cell replication, reducing the risk of cancer cell formation.

Ingredients
10 stems of young asparagus, trimmed
2 tablespoons of soya sauce or tamari
750 gm (26 oz) baby spinach, washed
150 gm (5¼ oz) sunflower seeds

For the dressing
Juice of 2 limes
2 tablespoons of extra virgin olive oil
1 teaspoons of wholegrain mustard
Ground black pepper

Method
Squeeze the lime juice into a small bowl. Put the remaining lime flesh and skins into a steamer with about 500 ml (18 fl oz) of water in the base. Add the asparagus and steam for 10 minutes (the flavour of the limes will infuse the asparagus). Remove from heat and plunge the asparagus immediately into cold water to prevent further cooking. They should still be bright green. Mix the sunflower seeds with the tamari and stand for 5–10 minutes to allow the seeds to absorb the sauce. Mix the ingredients for the dressing. Pour the dressing over the spinach and toss thoroughly. Arrange the asparagus over the leaves and sprinkle the seeds on top.

MUSHROOM AND BROCCOLI THAI STIR-FRY

Broccoli is considered to be one of the most important foods for preventing the development of cancer, as it is packed with antioxidant properties. It is part of the brassica family of vegetables which contain indoles (specific compounds believed to prevent potential cancer cells from replicating) You should try to include this vegetable in your diet several times per week. Shiitake mushrooms are rich in several anti-cancer properties. They are eaten regularly in Asian countries, where the levels of most of the common cancers are lower than in the Western world.

Ingredients

50gm (2 oz) of fresh or dried shiitake mushrooms

2 tablespoons of olive oil

3 cloves garlic, finely chopped

175 gm (6 oz) of broccoli (heads and stems separated) with stems sliced lengthways into thin slices

450 gm (16 oz) of tofu, drained and diced

240 gm (8½ oz) of chicken

2 tablespoons of light soy sauce

4 tablespoons of vegetable stock

1 tomato, skinned and chopped

1 teaspoon of corn flour

2.5 cm (1 in) length of fresh ginger, peeled and finely sliced lengthways

Method

If using dried mushrooms, cut them in half and soak for 30 minutes in a cup of warm water to rehydrate them. If using fresh, simply wipe clean (do not wash) and slice in half. Heat the oil gently in a wok or frying pan and add the garlic, ginger and chicken. Cook for 1 minute. then add the mushrooms (drain off the water if you soaked them) and the broccoli stems and florets. Stir and cook for a further minute. Then add the tofu, together with the soy sauce, vegetable stock and tomato. Mix, and then add the corn flour to thicken. Stir for a further minute, taking care not to break up the tofu. Serve immediately.

STUFFED TROUT WITH CITRUS AND ALMONDS

Trout is a good source of omega-3 essential fats, as are almonds which also contain leatrile which is thought to have anti-cancer properties. All citrus fruits are rich in vitamin C, one of the Fighting Five antioxidants nutrients.

Ingredients

4 rainbow or salmon trout (cleaned and gutted), approximately 225 gm (8 oz) each in weight

1 clove of garlic, peeled and crushed

2 shallots, peeled and finely diced

1 tablespoon of fresh parsley finely chopped

2 tablespoons of rice wine or dry white wine

Juice of 1 orange or 2 lemons

For the stuffing

60gm (2½ oz) ofwholemeal breadcrumbs

finely grated rind of ½ orange or lemon

1 small stick of celery, finely chopped

½ an apple, peeled, cored, and finely chopped

1 teaspoon of dried rosemary

1 tablespoon of low-fat natural yoghurt

Method   Rinse fish under running water and pat dry with a kitchen towel. Mix all the ingredients for the stuffing and fill each fish cavity from head to tail. Place the fish in a baking dish. Mix the orange or lemon juice with the rice wine or dry white wine, shallots, parsley and garlic and pour over the fish. Cover and cook in the oven at 180°C (350°F) for 25 minutes.

Serve with brown or wild rice, and steamed green vegetables such as broccoli, peas or spinach.

SWORDFISH OR HALIBUT WITH RED PEPPER SAUCE

Both these fish have excellent essential fatty acids from the omega-3 group, believed to protect cell membranes from damage, an important aspect of cancer prevention. If you have difficulty getting these fish you can use cod or haddock, but these tend to be lighter in taste. Red peppers are very rich in beta-carotene and vitamin C, which act as antioxidants.

Ingredients   4 swordfish steaks or halibut, or other fish of your choice
For red pepper sauce:
3 tablespoons of olive oil
3 large red peppers

4 cloves of garlic, peeled and chopped
1 medium onion, peeled and sliced
1½ tablespoons of balsamic vinegar
45 gm (1½ oz) of butter

Method   Rub olive oil over the peppers, and place in oven at 180°C (350°F) for 25 minutes until softened. Place in plastic bag, tie and leave for 20 minutes – this makes it easier to remove the unwanted skin from the peppers. Cut the peppers open and remove the skin, stems and seeds. Put into a food processor with the onions, garlic and olive oil and blend until smooth. Add the balsamic vinegar slowly (if added too fast, the sauce will curdle and separate) until completely mixed. Put the sauce into small saucepan and heat through while the fish is cooking.

To cook the fish, brush each side with a little olive oil and place under the grill for approximately 8–10 minutes on both sides (this will vary according to size and thickness of fish). You can judge when it is ready by inserting a knife into the fish – if it comes out clean, then the fish is cooked.

This dish would be delicious with a simple tossed mixed leaf salad.

glossary

Absorption The process by which nutrients are taken from the intestinal tract into the bloodstream, and into the cells in the body.

Allergen A substance (ingested or airborne) that promotes an allergic reaction.

Amino acid The breakdown product of protein. There are eight essential amino acids required by the body for rebuilding itself, which must be derived from the diet, as the body cannot make them itself.

Anaemia A condition that occurs when there are too few red blood cells in the body, or the haemoglobin levels are low (usually as a result of iron deficiency).

Anaemia (pernicious) Anaemia caused by vitamin B12 deficiency.

Angina Chronic chest pain and lack of ability to breath caused by a narrowing of the arteries leading to the heart.

Antacid Over-the-counter medication to lower the acid levels in the stomach.

Antibiotic Medication that destroys bacterial infection.

Antibody Part of the immune system that neutralises or engulfs invading pathogens.

Antigen An invader to the body that invokes an antibody reaction.

Antihistamine Medicinal or natural compound that prevents/suppresses the release of histamine.

Antioxidant A nutrient that slows the oxidative process caused by free radical action.

Arteriosclerosis The formation of plaque on the lining of the artery wall, caused by a build up of cholesterol and other lipids and debris.

Artery Blood vessels that carry oxygen away from the heart to the rest of the body.

Atherosclerosis A thickening of the arterial walls, which impairs blood flow.

Auto-immune disease Occurs when the body starts reacting to its own organ tissue – examples are rheumatoid arthritis, multiple sclerosis, systemic lupus and diabetes.

Bacteria Microscopic germs. Some are friendly, others harmful.

Benign Non-cancerous cells.

Beta-carotene A precursor to vitamin A.potent antioxidant.

Bile Secretion from the liver that helps break down fats in the digestive tract.

Bioflavonoid Compounds found just below the skin in fruits, that aid the absorption of Vitamin C.

Carcinogen Any cancer-causing agent

Cardiac Arrhythmia Irregular heartbeat.

Chemotherapy A treatment for cancer using chemicals to kill the cancer cells.

Cholesterol A natural fat manufactured by the body to transport fatty acids, involved in hormone production.

Co-enzyme A molecule required by an enzyme to perform its work in the body.

Required for the utilization of nutrients.

Complex carbohydrate Contains insoluble fibre within is structure, that slows down digestion.

Cruciferous Family of vegetables known to possess anti-cancer properties, e.g. broccoli, cabbage and cauliflower.

Detoxification Process of getting rid of toxic matter from the body.

Diuretic Any substance that increases the rate of urination. A process of elimination and detoxification.

DNA Deoxyribonucleic acid – the genetic coding found in the nucleus of every cell in the body, which determines specific characteristics and function in the body.

Endocrine Glands in the body that release hormone for control of specific functions e.g.ovaries, testes.

Endorphins Natural substance produced in the brain that has pain-killing properties.

Enzymes Molecules that break down proteins, involved in every reaction the body performs.

Essential fatty acids Substances that the body cannot manufacture by itself, that must be derived from the diet.

Free Radical A single atom that is not paired with another, causing an imbalance in the electron chemical reactions in the body. They are produced as a natural waste product in the body, as part of an end product of metabolism, as well as being found in oils that have been overheated, fatty foods, etc. Very damaging.

Fungus Single-cell organisms that feed off a host, e.g. Candida Albicans in the digestive tract.

Gas Excessive wind caused by bacterial or parasitic disturbance in the digestive tract.

Gastritis Inflammation of the stomach lining.

Gastroenteritis Inflammation of the stomach and intestines.

Gastrointestinal All parts of the digestive tract collectively.

Genetic Individual inherited characteristics.

Gland An organ that manufactures substances not required for its own metabolic activity.

Hair analysis Non-invasive test whereby a small quantity of hair is removed from the nape of the neck for analysis of minerals and potential toxic substances.

Haemoglobin Part of the red blood cell that carries oxygen. Iron dependent.

Hepatitis Inflammation of the liver.

Histamine A chemical that is released from the body tissues that exerts a reaction in the smooth muscle tissues, e.g. constriction of the nasal and bronchial passages in hayfever or a wheal on the skin.

Hormone An essential substance produced by the endocrine glands that regulate body functions.

Hydrochloric Acid Acid secreted in the stomach for the break down of proteins.

Hypertension High blood pressure.

Hyperallergenic Being very susceptible to allergic reaction.

Hypoallergenic Having little or no allergic reaction

Hypotension Low blood pressure.

Immune system The body's collective force for protection against invading pathogens.

Immunodeficiency Having low immune function.

Immunotherapy Techniques used to stimulate the function of the immune system.

Infection Disease caused by invading bacteria, viruses or fungi.

Insomnia The inability to sleep.

Insulin Hormone produced by the pancreas to regulate glucose metabolism.

Interferon A protein produced by the immune system to fight viruses, and protect uninfected cells.

Intestinal flora Friendly bacteria found in the intestinal tract.

Intrinsic Factor Compound produced in the stomach required for the absorption of vitamin B12.

Leukemia Cancer that causes overproduction of white blood cells.

Lipid Fat or fatty substance.

Lipoprotein A protein bound to a lipid. Aids in the transport of fats around the arterial and lymphatic systems.

Lymph A clear fluid that flows around the lymph vessels, alongside the arterial system. Important for collecting debris and unwanted matter to be removed from the body, as well as carrying nourishment to the tissues.

Lymph glands (or nodes) Areas where the lymph collects viral, bacterial and waste products for filtering and engulfing by the immune system.

Lymphocyte A type of white blood cell which forms part of the immune system.

Macrobiotic A dietary approach eliminating all animal produce and being highly alkaline in its vegetarian content.

Malabsorption Lack of absorption of nutrients from intestinal tract to bloodstream.

Malignant Containing cancerous cells.

Melanoma A malignant growth originating from pigment cells in the skin.

Menopause A slowing of the production of hormones that regulate menstruation, and eventual ceasing of the menses.

Metabolism The production of energy brought about in the cells as a result of the breakdown of nutrients to glucose.

Mucous Membrane The lining of any passage that has an opening to the outside of the body, e.g. ears, nose, moth, anus and vagina.

Naturopathy Healing practice using herbs, tonics and body alignment for the rebalancing of the body to allow to it

to heal itself.

Neurotransmitter A chemical that passes nerve impulses from one brain cell to another.

Nutrients Vital substances required by living beings for survival.

Oncogenes Cancer promoting cells.

Osteoporosis Softening of the bones from deterioration of the bone tissue.

Oxidation A chemical reaction that results from exposure to oxygen. Can b potentially harmful.

Parasite An organism that lives off another organism or host.

Pathogen Any microorgansim that causes disease, e.g. parasite.

Peroxides Free radicals that result fro the reaction between fats and oxygen.

Phagocytosis The engulfing of i nvading cells by immune cells to destroy them.

Polyunsaturated Fats Fats that are derived from vegetables and seeds, e.g flaxseed, sunflower and safflower oils. These oils should not be heated.

Prostaglandin A hormone-like substance that can promote or prevent inflammation.

Protein Complex compound formed from nitrogen which is essential to all living things. Required for growth and repair. Broken down into amino acids in the body.

Saturated fats Those fats that are derived from animal sources. Potentially damaging if overheated, and excessive amounts lead to arterioclerosi and obesity

Serotonin A neurotransmitter present nerve cells, required for relaxation, sleep and concentration.

Serum The clear coloured fraction of blood that carries the white and red blood cells.

Simple Carbohydrate Processed foods that yield simple sugars which are broken down rapidly into glucose.

Syndrome A group of symptoms that characterize specific disease.

T-cell An immune cell that is responsib for attacking invading pathogens.

Thrush Fungal infection caused by overgrowth of Cancida Albicans.

Toxicity A poisonous reaction in the body that results from an overload of toxins, and the body's inability to clear them efficiently.

Villi Minute finger-like projections found throughout the length of the digestive tract that absorb nutrients.

Virus A miniscule molecule that infects host cells. Can cause major illness. Not affected by antibiotics.

Vitamin Essential nutrients that the body cannot manufacture itself, and which must be derived from the diet.

Yeast A single cell organism that may cause infection in any canal of the body that is open to the outside, e.g. mouth, vagina and ears.

index

index

useful addresses

UK Organizations

British Diabetic Association
10 Queen Anne Street
London W1M 0BD
tel. 0171 323 1531

British Heart Foundation
14 Fitzhardings Street
London W1H 4DH
tel. 0171 935 0185

British Nutrition Foundation
52–54 High Holborn
London WC1V 6RQ
tel. 0171 404 6504

British Society for Mercury Free Dentistry
225 Old Brompton Road
London SW5 0EA
tel. 0171 373 3655

Coeliac Society
P.O. Box 220
High Wycombe
Buckinghamshire HP11 2HY
tel. 01494 437 278

Coronary Prevention Group
Suite 5/4
Plantation House
31/35 Fenchurch Street
London EC3M 3NN

Eating Disorders Association
Sackville Place
44 Magdalen Street
Norwich NR3 1JU
tel. 01603 621 414

Foresight
28 The Paddock
Godalming, Surrey GU7 1XD
tel. 01483 42 78 39

The Institute for Optimum Nutrition
Blades Court
Deodar Road
London, SW15 2NU
tel. 0181 877 9993

National Asthma Campaign
300 Upper Street
London N1
tel. 0345 010 203

National Eczema Society
Tavistock House
Tavistock Square
London WC1H 9SR
tel. 0171 388 4907

Society for the Promotion of Nutritional Therapy
P.O. Box 47
Heathfield
East Sussex
tel. 01825 872 921

The Soil Association
86 Colston Street
Bristol BS1 5BB
tel. 0117 929 0661

Vegetarian Society
Parkdale
Dunham Road
Altrincham
Cheshire WA14 4QG

World Cancer Research Fund
11–12 Buckingham Gate
London SW1E 6LB
tel. 0171 343 4200

US Organizations

American Association of World Health
1129–2012 st, NW, ste. 400
Washington DC 20036 3403

National Institute of Nutritional Education
1010 s. Jolier St
Aurora, CO 80012
(800) 530-8079

Useful Web Site Addresses

Austin Nutritional Research
www.realtime.net/anr/

Center for Nutritional Research
www.bovinecolostrum.com

Food and Nutrition Internet Navigator
www.fnii.ifis.org

International Food Information Service
www.ifis.org

Tufts University Nutrition Navigator
www.navigator.tufts.ed